II

The Goat Doctor of the Sierras

'A Healer of People'

by Gloria Hockensmith

The Goat Doctor of the Sierras

'A Healer of People'

First Printing

Cover: Goat Doctor photo by Leo Neibaur
Cover design by Robert Palitti

ISBN: 0-9711334-0-9

Gloriart Publishing Company

Printed in the United State of America

This book is dedicated to the memory of Franz Xavier Macek. Although known to many people in and around his home in Mosquito, California as Francis or Frank André, he was more widely known there and throughout the world as—

"The Goat Doctor"

VI

Introduction

"**M**rs. Moo Cow! I'd like you to set an appointment for Mrs. Martin for one day next week." A kind of half smile appeared on Mrs. Martin's face. She was too polite to comment on such a funny name, and myself, a very serious eighteen-year old, could not believe the doctor would joke with this poor woman who appeared in such pain as to be lucky to make it out the office door, let alone drive herself home!

It was 1951, and Dr. Yanis had recently employed me as a receptionist for his family practice in northeast Sacramento, California. The doctor, an Osteopath, Physician/Surgeon, was a highly intelligent, articulate professional man, albeit with a very active sense of humor! I became accustomed to being called: Mrs. Mud Hen, Mrs. Barnyard, and Mrs. Cattle Guard, along with his favorite of Mrs. Moo Cow, in his mischievous play on the name of Medcalf.

The doctor used these names often on his good humor days when all was right with the world, (his world that is). However, on his not so humorous days, if someone said or did something to annoy him (usually repeat offenders), he was apt as not to tell them exactly what he thought. He could be facetious and at times, got his point across in such an underhanded way; it took awhile before it registered on the poor soul that they had been at the brunt of his fury.

Such was the case of the unruly child brought to the office by his over-attentive mother for a scheduled vaccination. After much wiggling, wailing, and coaxing, the doctor managed to give the boy his injection. The minute the needle was out of the boy's rump, he jumped down from the examining table and with a swift kick nailed the doctor in his left shin.

After the blue air cleared and the mother finished professing her sorrow over the incident, the doctor smiled and said, "That's all right. Now if you'll just wait in the outer office for a minute or two." He had told the mother earlier he would give her the name of a dermatologist for a rash the boy had.

The doctor returned, handed the woman a business card and said, "This is the man I'd like you to take your son to, he could be of great help to you both, good day!"

Before the mother could say a word, Dr. Yanis slipped down the hall and into his office. The card was for a psychiatrist and on the back he had written, "This patient needs your help due to excessive mollycoddling!" Obviously, we never saw hide-nor-hair of them again!

Another day gone awry came about due to a patient again arriving late for her appointment. The doctor ushered the woman into his office and offered her the only other chair in the room, then seated himself at his desk and lit a cigarette.

The woman did a waving motion with her hand, as though to clear the air around her face. "I take it you do not care for my smoking," the doctor queried.

"I don't care for any cigarette or cigar smoke," she retorted.

This said, the doctor stood up, walked around from behind his desk and very politely said, "Well then, perhaps you'll do us both a favor and find yourself another doctor, one who doesn't smoke and doesn't mind your upsetting a whole day's schedule every time you have an appointment. Good Day!"

Now, the two aforementioned women had grated on his nerves more than once, and pretty much deserved what they received. I was, however, totally surprised and confused one day, when after treating a Mrs. Curtis for lower back pain, the doctor walked her to the outer door, held it open for her to exit and said in a stern voice, "If I were you, I'd go see the Goat Doctor!"

Mrs. Curtis had been in several times before and the doctor talked as though he liked her. He also appeared in good spirits just before her appointment. I wondered what in the world could she have said or done to incur his wrath, for him to tell her to go see "a goat doctor"? As bewildered as I was, I decided I was better off keeping my questions to myself.

My curiosity was sated a couple of days later when Mrs. Curtis returned. I learned Dr. Yanis had told her to stop by the office that day and he would have a map ready with instructions on how to get to a place, near Placerville where a man called "The Goat Doctor" lived.

Dr. Yanis confided to us that when a patient with a spine-related problem, such as Mrs. Curtis', did not respond to a set amount of treatments, he and several of his colleagues often referred many of their patients to "The Goat Doctor." He said the man was so-called because of the large herd of goats he kept that roamed all about his property.

I shall never forget the look on the face of this learned man, as he told us about the legendary man in the mountains. As he spoke, his shoulders seemed to inadvertently shrug and his face took on a gradual look of amazement. There was even an occasional shaking of his head as if in total disbelief of what he, himself, was telling us; about the various cases he knew of, where an incurable patient returned totally healed after seeing the Goat Doctor.

The doctor said because he had heard the Goat Doctor referred to as a "faith healer" he did not tell just anyone about him, only those he thought would have an open mind. He admitted, he himself was highly skeptical when he first heard of the man, but was now in complete awe of him! He confessed he had no idea what the man did that enabled him to cure so many people after trained medical practitioners had given up on them.

He told Mrs. Curtis a person had no way of knowing when he or she might be seen, as the Goat Doctor did not have set times for appointments and saw his patients on a first-come, first-served basis.

He suggested her chances of seeing him the same day would be better if she left her home in Carmichael (approximately fifty miles distance) by daybreak and during the middle of the week. He urged her to have her husband check the tires and brakes on their car, because it was a dangerously rough and winding canyon road. He also recommended they bring along food, drinks and blankets, in the event they had an over night wait.

Before long, a very happy and healthy Mrs. Curtis stopped by the office to thank Dr. Yanis for referring her to the Goat Doctor. She bubbled about her experience there. She described their scary automobile trip, the rustic old cabin with animals all around the place, and the treatment she received. She told of all the people entering the cabin in wheelchairs, on crutches and stretchers, who came walking out on their own!

Throughout the subsequent years, I continued to hear unbelievable tales about the Goat Doctor. The stories left me with an unflagging interest and curiosity to learn more about this remarkable man. I often asked in bookstores and libraries, if there was a book on "The Goat Doctor." Always, the answer was no!

Finally–having the time–I decided I would endeavor to research and record for posterity; everything I could find about this mysteries man.

I have spent the past seven years; searching (driving 830 miles for one interview alone), then weighing, evaluating, and piecing together Goat Doctor stories from several hundred people. I gleaned information from his patients, friends, neighbors, doctor, and lawyer, as well as from newspapers, magazines, and legal records.

Stories that include the names of people now deceased came from letters—saved by people throughout the years and some came from written and/or taped interviews taken by various people who started the book long ago.

The Goat Doctor's life is in chronological order, however for continuity that in no way change the facts, some individual accounts and statements are not in sequence of years, but are placed where they involve a specific topic.

I do not purport to be a writer or a historian. As an artist, using the information given me, I have strived to paint with words as complete and accurate a picture as possible of this extraordinary man – "The Goat Doctor of the Sierras"

G. Hockensmith

XII

Acknowledgments

I am indebted to literally hundreds of people.

First off, I credit Pat Jones, gone, but not forgotten, author of the books "Colfax" and "Chicago Park" for encouraging me to write the book.

For getting me started with valid information, I give special thanks to Lois Pearson. Lois, who knew the Goat Doctor longer and better then anyone else, not only shared with me what she knew, she put me in touch with others who knew him well and continued to be on call throughout the years to answer questions and give advise.

To my good friend Mary Moga go my sincerest thanks, respect, and admiration for fulfilling the almost impossible task of sticking with me until completion of the book. Her input, patience, and support were invaluable while working as my gal Friday/computer person.

My appreciation and gratitude to dear friends Betty and Bill Lawler; Phyllis Gernes, author "Hidden in the Chaparral"; and Alton Pryor, author "Outlaws and Gunslingers", for sharing their valuable opinions, time, and encouragement while editing the book.

I thank Jim (Sierra) Normandi of White's Electronics, in San Raphael; Walt Wiley and J. J. Brown with the Sacramento Bee; Candice Packard of The Evergreen Herb Garden in Mosquito and Jo Thomas with the Mosquito Byte for their help in acquiring needed information.

Of the twenty-three people who said they started to write the book, I am especially indebted to the following two:

Dr. D. Polley of Fair Oaks, California interviewed several of the Goat Doctor's closest friends and neighbors for his intended book in 1982. However, soon after he began writing, his chiropractic practice became overly busy and the book was set aside. Dr. Polley felt as strongly as I that the book should be written, and was anxious to share with me the audiotapes he had made of the sessions.

Elaine Kamp of Midvale, Utah, started a book about the Goat Doctor while living in Placerville, California, in the 1980's. She had to give it up after moving out of state. Elaine heard I was writing the book and sent me copies of her notes on the information she had gathered from people, along with a few pictures.

To the many people, who assisted in my research at the El Dorado Court House; the Placerville Hall of Records and Museum; the Placerville and Sacramento Library; the Auburn and Sacramento Mormon Family Center and the Sacramento Bee, thank you again.

If a story appears to be that of one person but has another person's name to it, it could be because many stories were virtually identical. I received anywhere from ten to a hundred individual accounts, about; the rough road, the scary bridge, the huge vegetable garden, Frank's healings, his looking like Jesus, Anna being clairvoyant, the buried money, etc. etc.

I must also point out, because computers have a mind (?) of their own, people's names and initials may have been inadvertently changed, dropped, or misplaced. I wish to apologize in case of <u>any</u> errors in this regard.

I still have questions I would like answers to and I am sure there are some things the reader would like explained, but—I can only tell you, that which was told to me by those who knew Frank Andre'.

It is regrettable that the book was not written years ago, so more of Anna and Frank's remedies and methods could have been saved. Evidently, people were so in awe of the man and the atmosphere of the place, that is what their memories chose to retain and his remedies became secondary.

"My memories of the Goat Doctor stories are like jewels in my memory bank. He was mystical and mysterious, but not mythical. He was real and should be put in a place of honor—his rightful place in history. He was an integral part of the romance of the west. It's time for him to be remembered."

J. Scribner

XVI

The

Goat Doctor

of the Sierras

'A Healer of People'

XVIII

Chapter One

In a remote area on a snow-covered mountain in Austria, a small child was found wandering alone by a man and his wife while skiing. In an effort to find the boy's family, the couple posted notices on trees and buildings in several villages. They remained in the area for weeks searching for information without any luck. They then took the child home to rear as their own.

It is unknown if Franz Xavier Macek was the boy's birth name or a name given by the family who raised him. Little is known of his younger years; other than he lived in Czechoslovakia some of the time and that after completing his schooling, he found employment as a waiter in an elegant restaurant in Vienna.

As far back as he could remember Franz's adoptive parents encouraged him to leave Europe as soon as he could. The people of Austria were suffering from famine and political uprisings were prevalent throughout the country.

After both of his adoptive parents died, Franz wrote to family friends in San Francisco, California, telling of his desire to come to America. He received a return letter inviting him to stay at the couple's home until he became situated and able to provide for himself.

With a modest inheritance and money saved from his restaurant earnings Franz amassed the amount needed for passage, plus, what he thought to be enough to tide him over until he found work in America. He was nineteen years of age when he arrived in the United States in 1907.

> *It was while traveling across the United States, that I first felt the sensation–as though hands were on my shoulders guiding me.*   **F. Macek**

Franz was bitterly disappointed when he arrived in San Francisco. It was upsetting to see the city in ruin from the devastating earthquake of 1906. Also, in searching for his friends, he found the charred remains of their home, but was unable to find them.

It was an especially difficult time for everyone. The majority of businesses had been demolished, the cost of everything inflated beyond reason, and there was little work to be found. It was even harder for Franz to find employment because his native tongue was German and he spoke little English.

After much thought, he decided to start his own business of selling vegetables. By the time he bought a horse, wagon, and supplies, there was little money left, but at least he had a way of making a living.

> "Something he said that I thought very interesting was that when he bought the fresh vegetables and fruits to sell on his route, whatever amount of food he bought, was always just right—he never had any leftovers at the end of the day."   **E. Clark**

In 1908, while selling produce door to door, Franz stopped at the home of Ernest and Anna André. When Anna answered the door, there was an immediate feeling of closeness between them.

"The minute they met at her door, she looked at him and he looked at her, and she said, 'You've come.' And he said, 'Yes, I am here.' He said he felt instantly that was where he belonged." **E. Clark**

During another stop at the Andrés, he met Anna's husband Ernest. The three got along well and soon Franz was a frequent guest for dinner. However, within a few weeks of their meeting, he began feeling ill. Each day he tired a little earlier as his health continued to worsen. Barely able to care for his horse, his route gradually shortened to a few blocks, which did not include the Andrés' home. Finally, unable to earn enough to cover his rent, he began sleeping on the beach.

The Andrés wondered what had happened to their young friend when he inexplicably stopped coming to their home. Their paths met again one day when Ernest and Anna were walking along the shore and came across a cold, wet, and hungry Franz. He was skin and bones and appeared to be dying. They were shocked at seeing him in such bad condition.

They took him to their home for a hot meal and dry clothes. As they sat and visited, Franz told them for the first time of his plight since arriving in America: how he could not find the friends who had promised their love and support, about finding the remains of their home, and how he wished he could find out if they were still alive.

Anna's heart went out to the young man, so ill and alone in the world and she told Ernest the prediction Edgar Cayce, the famous psychic, gave her when she was a young woman.

"Anna, you will never have any children of your own, but a son will be sent to you from across the waters, and you will do great work together."

E. Cayce

Convinced Cayce's prediction had come true, Anna talked it over with Ernest, and he agreed that Franz should move in with them and be part of their family. This was quite gesture on their part as they were in the midst of large adjustments.

The recently married, middle-aged couple (each 40) had barely moved to San Francisco when Anna was in an accident that caused injury to her back. A few weeks later the earthquake struck, burying Ernest in the rubble of a building. By the time rescuers got to him, almost a week later, his brown hair had turned completely white. The couple was still recovering from their injuries and adjusting to their environment where the very earth and surroundings had drastically changed.

Anna took Franz to her doctor who diagnosed him with tuberculosis and confined him to a sanitarium in southern California. The doctors there told the Andrés once Franz was well enough to leave the hospital, he should live where the air was clean and fresh, away from the city and preferably at a higher elevation.

Ernest and Anna had been looking at property in the mountains before the earthquake, in anticipation of where they would live after retiring. Earlier than planned, spurred on by their intense desire to help Franz, they purchased property in Mosquito, a small settlement in the foothills of the Sierra Mountains.

Located in the Mother Lode, between Placerville ("Hangtown") and Coloma, California, Mosquito was in a sparsely populated area that boasted of a Post Office and a one-room schoolhouse. Gold was found in Coloma 1848, and soon after in nearby Mosquito Canyon. It was due to prospectors that Mosquito was so named.

"Some miners were sitting around a campfire one night discussing things in general, and at one point, the topic turned to thoughts of giving a name to the area in which they lived. I guess their feeling was that it had to be called something. One miner came up with the idea that the next word anybody said aloud - would be the name used. At that moment, someone slapped his arm and said 'damn mosquitoes', and they couldn't call it 'Damn' could they?"

L. Beckett-Pearson
Mosquito Memories – L. Davies

The original deed to the property, filed at the request of Ernest André on August 1, 1911, identifies Annie Elizabeth Schwartz as owner.

Mosquito Road divided the André's property. On a hill on one side of the road was a house, average for the area, painted white with steps that led up to a porch, which extended across the entire front of the house. Behind the house, next to a large wooden shed, was a pump that drew water from a fresh mountain spring.

About a quarter-mile beyond the house, parallel with the road but on the other side, was a garage. Behind the garage (used as a barn), the land continued a downward slope to the bottom of the hill to Mosquito Creek.

Ernest and Anna (he always called her "Annie" or "Mother") visited the property they dubbed "Andréville" a few times the first year. On each of these visits, they brought along a few fruit trees to plant.

By most accounts, it was 1912, when Ernest took an early summer vacation, and he and Anna spent their first two weeks on the property. During this time, on the south side of a hill on the other side of Mosquito Creek, in the only location suitable for a garden, Ernest turned the soil and he and Anna planted a vegetable garden.

Anna stayed on in Mosquito to maintain the garden in preparation of Franz's release from the hospital, while Ernest returned to San Francisco alone in order to work to pay off the Andréville mortgage.

Due to cost and distance, it was several months between Anna's visits to Franz. She knew his recovery would take time, but after her second visit, she became very upset. It was obvious he was in no better shape than when he entered the hospital and in fact, he looked sicker.

Confident that he would be better off in her care than in the overcrowded hospital, with its undermanned and overworked staff, Anna asked to take him home. The doctors said they could not allow it because he was contagious.

Determined to get Franz out, she began a campaign barraging the various heads of the hospital with letters assuring them that he would be a threat to no one if they allowed her to take him to his new home, far out in the country, where, except for herself, he would be completely alone.

After doctors had surgically removed one lung and found the other spotted with TB, Anna was informed that since they did not expect Franz to live beyond two to three months and provided she kept him totally isolated as promised, she could take him home.

Along with Franz's change of environment from southern California to Mosquito, came another change—that of his name. Using derivations of his German name Franz, and taking his foster parents' surname, he became Francis or Frank André. More commonly referred to as Frank, except by Anna and Ernest who always called him André.

When I first arrived in Mosquito, I was dying. Then one day I felt the sensation as though I had a scale on my chest and it could tip either way–I could live or die. I made a vow in prayer that if I lived I would spend the rest of my life helping humanity.

Frank André

Anna always kept a safe distance from Frank so as not to contract the disease and reminded him daily to keep away from people. Not only could he spread the disease, she told him in his weakened state he was highly susceptible to any virus others might have.

In her determination to heal her foster son, one of the first things Anna did was buy some goats. She believed goat milk and goat meat, along with fresh fruits and vegetables, were the best food sources for a healthy body.

Adamant in her belief that Frank should "live as one with nature" to regain his health; wearing only a loincloth, he was to live outdoors winter and summer, sleeping outside on the ground at night or in the barn with the goats. Anna believed that touching and smelling the oil in goat fur, especially angora, had a healing effect.

"Let your hair grow long," she told him. "It conducts electricity and gives you energy." She urged him to go barefoot, making direct contact with the soil to receive the healing powers from the earth.

Anna would not allow Frank to do anything but rest and he was far too weak to do otherwise, as she worked from dawn to dusk caring for him, the goats, and the garden.

Each morning after her breakfast, selected from Indian corn, pine nuts, acorns, rice or other grains, fruit from their trees, wild berries and goat's milk, she filled a basket with food for Frank.

She then pumped a bucket of water and carried it and the basket of food down to the barn where she poured half of the water into a pan for Frank to cleanse his self and the rest she used to wash the nanny goats' udders. While Frank ate his breakfast, Anna did the milking, then turned the goats out to roam, and swept out the barn.

Returning to the house with the milk, her next chore was to walk back down the hill behind the barn, wade across Mosquito Creek and tend the vegetable garden. She tilled the soil, weeded and thinned plants, picked the ripe vegetables, then irrigated the garden by carrying buckets of water from the creek.

This done, she once again returned to the house with the vegetables and prepared their lunch. Goat meat, chicken, fish, eggs, or cottage cheese made from goat's milk, constituted a large part of their diet, along with vegetables and wheat bread.

After lunch and a short rest, she again pumped buckets of water as needed to bathe, clean house, wash clothes or for cooking.

The goats gradually returned to the barn in the late afternoon (sometimes needing to be rounded up) and Anna once again washed and milked the nannies. Due to the prevalence of coyotes, the goats had to be secured for the night.

Frank and Anna enjoyed visiting with one another after their evening meal, and never seemed to run out of conversation. He still had a strong German accent and Anna spent hours helping him perfect his English.

When Ernest was able to make the long arduous trip from San Francisco to Mosquito, he would do the more laborious tasks such as digging trenches the size of small bathtubs. He piled the earth next to the hole, convenient for Anna to alternate shoveling dirt and pouring in water, combining the two until the mud was about the consistency of a thick pancake batter.

She had Frank remove his loincloth and lower himself into the mud bath until only his head was above ground. "The wet earth will draw out the impurities that sicken you and the minerals will heal you," she explained. He often soaked for as long as half-a-day.

Passersby were frequently startled seeing a head with long, thick, dark wavy hair appearing to be growing out of the ground.

"Mrs. Andre' also took sunbaths in hollowed out depressions in red clay on the southern side of the hill this for health."   **E. M. Bliss**

Anna scraped a shallow nest-like hollow in the ground and lined it with fresh pine needles to make a comfortable bed for Frank's afternoon naps. "The turpentine in the needles," she told him, "are medicinal, and heal many ailments."

Frank spent most of his days, for many months, soaking in mud baths and lying on his bed of pine needles.

Just as his strength had left him years before, it now began to return, ever so slowly. Anna's hopes grew as she watched him gain in weight and energy. Invariably though, she had to endure the upset as his health again declined.

The relapses went on for months, which were to make up years, before Anna's care finally had the positive effect she had worked so hard to achieve.

Although Frank's five-foot seven-inch frame was still on the delicate side, he now retained his gained weight, color returned to his face and he was able to be up and around for longer periods of time; without becoming breathless and exhausted.

He began walking with Anna when she herded the goats to fresh pasture. If he grew tired she scraped the ground with a hoe, just enough to clear off the grass and loosen the dirt for him to lie down and make contact with the earth while he rested.

It was a day of joy when Frank was able to walk with Anna to the vegetable garden, bend down, and pull a few weeds.

"He was wearing a loincloth when I first saw him.
I used to take walks along Mosquito Creek and I
would see him down there working in the garden.

"At that time the garden was a long way from
their house, maybe a half a mile. This was the period
of time when he was still trying to get back his
health, although you'd never have known he'd been so
sick. He was always as brown as a nut."

L. Beckett-Pearson

Anna encouraged Frank to take daily walks by himself
for exercise. There were few people in the area at the time
and she felt he should be able to avoid them. However, he
must have hungered for the company of others, as people
began seeing him traipsing along in the same direction,
hiding behind trees and bushes, peeking out at them.

Wearing only a loincloth, at a quick glimpse, he appeared
to be naked and with his dark brown hair hanging below the
middle of his back (unheard of in those days), he often
scared people.

"When the Andrés first came to Mosquito, people
called Frank, 'The Crazy Man'." **E. Fossati**

"I remember people calling Frank the 'Wild Man of
the Mountain'." **J. Jordon**

"He was called 'The Nature Faker' for years."

E. M. Bliss

When a passer-by happened along the road, Anna would
sometimes walk out and greet them to chat awhile. Often as
not, the person was taken aback within the first few
minutes of conversation.

Where most people, upon greeting, asked, "How are you?" Anna usually told them how they were. When she said to them, "You are looking well," they could be sure they were without some hidden ailment. She instinctively knew if a person had a medical problem just by looking at them.

She often answered a person's question even before they asked it. One day, she was sitting on her porch when a neighbor stopped by to say hello and to ask the time.

The woman said, "Hello! I wonder..."

"It's 2:30," Anna replied.

The woman next started to ask the name of a plant she noticed in the yard. Anna told her the name before she could get the question out.

The strangeness of the conversation began to register on the woman just as she was about to leave. As they said their good-byes and the visitor started walking toward the road, Anna called to her.

"Congratulations".

"What for?" the woman asked.

"For the baby you are expecting," Anna replied.

This was a total surprise to the woman. She was not aware she was pregnant. As it turned out, Anna was right.

Not only could Anna tell the well being of a person, their past, and their future, she could give news about people nearby or faraway. She was clairvoyant.

It was second nature for her to say aloud what her sixth sense told her, but it was far too much for many of the locals to understand. Some were afraid of her and a few called her a witch. Indeed, she was fortunate the era of burning witches at the stake was a thing of-the-past, as she most likely would have been a prime candidate.

Life can be very unpleasant for newcomers moving into an established neighborhood, especially if they do not fit the mold the natives have set for them. Not only did the Andrés not fit the mold, they were drastically different from anyone around.

They were oblivious of the fact that they were setting tongues a-wagging and that they were at the butt of many a joke, but they were aware of being shunned.

Anna could not understand why people turned and walked the other way when they saw her coming, or why so many people would not return her friendly wave as they passed their place. Albeit, when she waved at those people she was often buck-naked!

"A couple of times driving past their place, we saw Mrs. André out in their yard naked as a jaybird. Once, she was hanging clothes on the line, without a stitch on and she just waved to us, as if there was nothing at all unusual about it."   **L. Croft**

"People were always gossiping about the Andrés. They thought Frank and Anna were nuts. At one point, they were really up in arms and threatening to call the authorities on Anna.

"It was because Frank was seen chopping wood out in two feet of snow, wearing only a loincloth, no shoes or shirt!

"The wood was for the mother's wood-burning stove, but he wasn't allowed inside the house. She made him sleep in the animal shed in a pit filled with soiled straw—goat dung and all."   **Anonymous**

The Andrés became rich fodder for the gossips. It took little imagination for people to come up with the names of "The Wild Man" or "The Crazy Man," as Frank's appearance did fit the description. However, Frank was as far from crazy and wild as Anna was of being weird or dumb, as some were labeling her. She may have come across as spooky or weird but she was definitely not dumb.

"Anna was a very smart woman. One of the negative problems was that people around here were conservative and a lot of them were threatened by Frank and Anna's intelligence and sensitivity. That's why they were so opposed to them. They didn't want anybody stirring their stagnant pool."   **C. Neilsen**

Anna Elizabeth Raker [André] was born in Mifflinberg, Pennsylvania, on May 3, 1865. Her parents, John and Caroline Raker, were prominent upper class. The entire family was intelligent and worldly. In 1873, the family moved to northern California.

Anna was politically minded and informed people her brother was John E. Raker, an attorney in Susanville who became a district attorney in Modoc County, California, a judge of the Superior Court and a California Congressman. She kept apprised of world situations through newspapers and journals and never hesitated voicing her opinions. She wrote scathing letters to politicians when she did not like their views.

"She gave my brother letters to mail. Mrs. André wrote to County officials and even world leaders! Local women received letters too!

"They were not accepted by the community because it was a platonic relationship. [Some people thought Anna and Frank to be a couple.] None of the women around here would have anything to do with her."   **E. M. Bliss**

"Frank's mother used to have my husband mail letters to people all over the United States." **D.Cupps**

Anna's bedroom contained the remnants of her past; the items she held most dear and had managed to salvage throughout the years. The vases, figurines, pictures, fine linens, and curtains all permeated the atmosphere of old wealth.

A large bookcase held the extensive collection of books she had brought to Mosquito. As a history buff, at least half of her books dealt with that subject. She had a variety of books for children and many books about herbs and foods she enjoyed studying. A smaller bookcase in the room held a collection of Zane Grey westerns.

"Anna Andre' told me Zane Grey was a relative of hers. She told me he sent her all of his books to read and she was to title them for him or to give him her opinion on a title he had made up. Then he would sign and send her one of the first (printed) copies of each book." **L. Croft**

"Anna was a real nut over her Zane Grey books. She claimed she was a relation to Zane Grey. Whether she was or not, we don't know. We never had any proof, but then we never had any reason to doubt her." **L. Beckett-Pearson**

"We never called Frank's mother Anna, she was always Mother André, and Ernest was always called Dad. We lived near the Andrés and used to visit with Mother André in her room. We behaved like normal kids, but not in Mother André's room.

"There were special things in her room that made me feel like I was in the presence of a queen. She showed culture. Her library covered one entire wall of her bedroom.

"She had the full series of Grace Livingston Hill and Elsie Dinsmore girls books. She would occasionally allow me and a few other children to take one of her storybooks home for a few days. I know

Mother André had a complete set of Zane Grey books. I'm pretty sure they were first editions." **C. Neilsen**

"Mrs. André was a handsome, intelligent woman. When I first met her, she was a slender lady—about five-foot eight-inches tall. She had gray hair and wore long skirts or full length dresses in floral print, colorful but not gaudy. She often wore a sweater or shawl." **O. Beckett**

On May 21, 1915, Anna Elizabeth André Schwartz signed an indenture giving Ernest Frank Schwartz André and Franz Xavier André Macek two-thirds interest in the property. [sic]

During World War I, newspapers and posters spread the warning "Guard your words—the enemy may be listening." Anyone with so much as a trace of a German accent could be suspect as a spy and deported.

Frank was facing deportation when Anna and Ernest first took him in because either he had failed to register at the immigration office within a required date or, his allotted time in this country had run out.

To avoid deportation it was common practice for un-naturalized citizens to change their name through adoption, marriage, and/or withdraw from the system by moving far away from the immigration department. As to moving far away—it is doubtful anyone could have found a more remote or isolated place to live.

There was only one road into the small settlement of Mosquito and it was unbelievably treacherous. A newsletter put out at the time by Michigan Cal Lumber Company described the trip from Placerville to Pino Grande. Mosquito was midway, nine miles east of Placerville. The article warned, "Never attempt the trip through the rugged canyons and eternal hills across the South Fork of the American River with other than an experienced driver."

The write-up suggested, "Allow time to navigate because of the sharp, hazardous grades, and hairpin turns. A single false move, bursting of a tire, a slip of the brake, could hurl the vehicle two thousand feet straight down into the leaping, dashing and splashing waters of the American River. As you continue down the narrow roadway, you eventually come to a thin cable bridge that crosses the river some three hundred feet below."

The cable bridge measured nine feet seven inches wide and one hundred forty-one feet long. Ranchers and miners built it in 1867. It had no side rails and when one end went down, the other end went up. It was literally a swinging bridge!

Mosquito Bridge

After crossing the bridge then ascending the canyon wall a mile and a half, the one-lane Mosquito Road led to the André Ranch. The rough road was called many different names such as "Suicide Road" and "Corkscrew Road".

"The roads in the area were like cow paths, much like the back roads in Korea—not for the timid soul!"
G. Milham-Desjardin

"The road was very narrow and winding and there were only a couple of places to stop. Anybody driving up or down the steep hill had to blow their horn, so when you heard it, **whoever** was near a place to stop, did!" **W. Durfey**

"It's wilderness now, but at the time, it was REALLY wilderness. The road out to the Andrés place was like 'The Burma Road' because of all the switchbacks." **D. Dodge**

"What a trip over that cable suspension bridge and the eight miles of serpentine road." **T. Hendricks**

———

Sometime around 1917, that Anna deemed Frank well and allowed him to be around other people. With the gradual return of his strength, he began a project he thought of utmost importance—the building of a large dray wagon.

When asked why he was building such a contraption, he would reply, "Because we want to be prepared in case of an invasion."

"But the war is being fought in Europe, not here," people tried to tell him, sometimes walking away, shaking their heads muttering, "What will those Andrés be doing next?"

Perhaps Frank's fear stemmed from his childhood, but Anna also felt they were going to be invaded. When sitting out doors, her gaze was never still as her eyes glanced from here to there in searching the hills.

Frank and Anna stocked the dray wagon with canned goods, dried foods, pots and pans, blankets and other essentials. For years, they stayed prepared to move higher into the mountains at a moments notice.

After the wagon was completed, Frank and Anna started construction of a log cabin. It was about 50 yards below the country road, on a plot of land nestled in a densely wooded area, across the road, and approximately a mile from Anna's house. Frank hewed the logs by cutting and stripping trees on their property and used mules to move them in place.

The land was level at the entry of the twenty by twenty-four foot cabin, then sloped downhill toward the back. There was a door and a couple of small windows on the front of the cabin and two or three small windows on the sidewalls. On the back wall of the room to the right of a large stone fireplace was a door to a small porch with six or seven steps that led down to an outhouse. A short distance down the hill behind the cabin and outhouse was Mosquito Creek.

"Myself, a friend, and my brother and sister, had gone out hunting. As we passed Frank's place, he came out and invited us to tea.

"He appeared to be living alone in a cabin-like house. It was one large room. In one corner was his bed. He had made the furniture himself out of manzanita. It was quite beautiful. I remember the chairs had cushions covered in goatskin. The seat had straps of goat leather woven together and tacked on to give spring to it. There were many goat pelts used for rugs. Everything was very neat.

"We liked him right off. People who didn't know him gossiped awful about him because he dressed different."   **T. Harper**

Frank became well acquainted with the man from whom Anna bought their goats and goat meat. He taught Frank how to butcher, skin, and tan the hides of the goats and Frank saw this as a way to make an income to help Ernest with the mortgage and taxes on the property.

For years, Anna sold any extra vegetables they had to passers-by in an effort to supplement their income. After buying more goats, she and Frank planted more fruit trees, enlarged the vegetable garden, and placed a sign along the road offering fruits, vegetables, goat milk, and goat meat for sale.

While selling their products, Anna found most people knew little about vitamins and minerals needed for a healthy body. She knew a lot about this subject and enjoyed advising her customers as to what foods or herbs were good for a particular health problem.

As more people began coming to her for advice, Anna decided to start a study group, to further share what she knew about the health benefits of natural foods and herbs.

Below is a copy of the calling card Anna gave out at this time.

MRS. ANNA E. ANDRÉ

WESTERN REPRESENTATIVE OF

THE INTERNATIONAL PURITY ASSOCIATION

PLACERVILLE, CALIFORNIA

MOSQUITO DISTRICT

Because of her psychic ability, Anna continually came across strange to most anyone who met her, but in time, as people saw her predictions come true, they recognized her for the intelligent woman she was.

"Mother André was very psychic. She told us that she had a direct line and guide and her guide told her what to do. That was the process, by which, they came up here and found the land they bought. She said she was guided to get the goats, particularly the Angoras.

"If Mother André liked you, you could come to her and ask her about a health problem, or if whatever you were going to do would be a good thing or not, if it would be successful or a failure. She would tell us children whether we should do something or not. Her advice was always sound.

"She used to tell people where to prospect for gold or to dig a well for water. She was able to tell people if their mining claim was worth working by the ore samples they brought to her. She was very apt. She didn't call it a séance or any of the fancy words that we use today and she didn't go into a trance.

"If she didn't like someone, she would bluntly tell them to go away, saying she didn't know anything. I saw her turn people away saying, 'No, I'm not interested in what you're doing!'" **C. Neilsen**

"The main thing I think about Anna was she was very psychic. Ernest and Frank catered to her with great respect. Ernest usually called her Annie and Frank called her Mother or Mumsy Dear."
V. Alexander

"I talked with his mother several times and she told me things about myself no one else could have known. I felt her power as a psychic."
G. Bottenberg

"We met Mother André two or three years after they moved to Mosquito. We were witness to her psychic abilities often.

"At the time, there was very little traffic in the area. While visiting with Mother Andre' one evening, my husband said, 'I wonder if there will be anyone else driving through Mosquito tonight.'

"I happened to look over at Anna and saw her normal expression change. All at once, she seemed to be in a semi-trance. I can only describe it as staring into space.

"It was for just a moment or so before she said, 'Yes, there is a car on the way. It will be here at such and such a time.' Sure enough, she was right, but then she always was!" **M. Waggersman**

"On my husband's first visit there he met the mother, and as they were talking, she told him the brakes were not set on the car. He went back up the hill and found that was so." **R. Maguire**

"I knew Mrs. André and she was possessed of second sight!" **E. M. Bliss**

———————

While living alone in San Francisco, Ernest taught himself shorthand and to use the typewriter and filled his free hours doing what he enjoyed most—writing poems and short stories.

He began free-lancing his works with local newspapers and magazines. Even the San Francisco Examiner accepted his write-ups. The best known of his short stories was one titled "Boston".

He and Anna stayed in close touch through letters. Ernest admired, respected, and encouraged Anna in her work. She inspired him to write the following poem:

Sister Anna

Coming to another milestone on the rugged road of life,
We salute a loving mother and an ever faithful wife.
Handicapped by natal weakness, she has fought a valiant fight.
On the side of truth and justice, battling always for the right.

As bread cast upon the waters comes back after many days,
So her many deeds of kindness through unknown and hidden ways
Have returned with added blessings and expressive words of love
That reflect the Everlasting Almoner who dwell above.

Unaffected by the ravages of Time's relentless hand,
Shines the incorporeal spirit no condition can command;
Seeing far beyond the signs of wrinkled brow or silvery hair,
We behold the radiant Presence ever young and bright and fair.

When the mortal strength is failing in the struggle to attain,
She relies upon The Highest, and has never called in vain.
We recall, on one occasion, when her spirit winged its flight
To a higher plane of being, girdled by celestial light.

Dowered with discrimination and an occult psychic power,
We rely on her to guide us, and select the pliant hour.
With a natural clairvoyance she foresees the coming time
When the shadows have departed, and we enter Life Sublime!

Chapter Two
1920 - 1929

Frank and Anna were still living alone on the Mosquito property when the Fourteenth Census of the United States was taken on January 5, 1920. It records Frank M. André as head of household, age 30; single, occupation farmer; year of immigration to the United States, 1907; alien, born in Austria; language, German; Father's birthplace, Munich, Germany; mother's birthplace, Munich, Germany. It lists Anna E. André as mother, age 54.

On May 9, 1921, Ernest Frank Schwartz André, Anna Elizabeth André Schwartz (aka Annie Elizabeth Schwartz), and Franz Xavier André Macek signed another indenture to the André property that returned sole ownership to Anna Elizabeth André. [sic]

Anna now had eight to ten regular members in her "International Purity Association" group, who met every other week at her house.

Often during the meetings, someone would have an ailment or injury. Anna would usually recommend herbal cleansers, astringents, poultices, or ointments for external problems. For internal ailments, she advised special diets and/or herbal teas.

If their problem involved muscle pains she had them lie on a makeshift treatment table, located in one of the bedrooms. For these patients, she did what she called "soft massage." After each treatment, Anna had the group form a circle around the patient and said a prayer for their recovery.

"In the beginning it was Anna who began the practice of caring for people, her treatment being a combination of manipulation and prayer." **O. Beckett**

People who witnessed a healing session, in which Anna cured someone, could not help but praise her. Many of these people began calling her a "Faith Healer." However, it was all hocus-pocus to the local troublemakers. They ignored the good she did and took glee in adding "charlatan" and "quack" to the other demeaning names they called her.

Frank was in awe of Anna's healing and psychic abilities and wanted to learn all he could from her. She began teaching him the art of meditation.

"It is not only conducive to good health," she explained, "but it will stimulate your sixth sense."

"She sensed in her young adopted son a power greater than her own and took it upon herself to develop and nurture these abilities." **Peg Presba**
Georgetown Gazette

Anna taught Frank her techniques for massage and soon he was helping her give treatments. He became engrossed in the subject. He wanted to learn everything he could about the anatomy of the human body, especially anything to do with the relationship of the spine in connection with the functions of the organs.

"He told me, while butchering the goats, that he studied their skeletons in teaching himself how to touch and feel for bone structure."   **O. Beckett**

In his quest to learn more, Frank decided to look up Oscar Pinneo, an old gentleman friend who for a time occupied the bed next to his in the tuberculosis sanitarium. He and Oscar had stayed in touch through letters and Oscar told Frank he practiced what he called 'osteopatic' medicine.

After his release from the hospital, Oscar moved to Auburn, California and set up practice. This ad is from the Auburn Blue Book – 1914:

Dr. O. E. Pinneo
OSTEOPATIC PHYSICIAN
Office at Residence of Mrs. S. Locher

Phone, Black 316

"My Uncle, Dr. Pinneo, was like a chiropractor, although I don't think he had a license of any kind. He lived in Auburn before he moved to Placerville. As I recall, he became disenchanted with Auburn after the 'city fathers' pretty much ran him out of town."

D. Howell

In Placerville, Oscar opened "The Candy Kitchen," a combination ice cream parlor, soda fountain, and candy store on Main Street. Above the Candy Kitchen were two rooms he used surreptitiously for treating patients.

Frank visited Oscar who welcomed him and willingly instructed him in his method of manipulation. In exchange, Frank did odd jobs for him. Through Dr. Pinneo he was able to order medical journals and books.

He had no problem with the sharp hairpin curves on Mosquito Road because he traversed it by foot—barefoot, that is. He walked the 18 miles to Placerville and back, three or four days a week, for nearly a year.

> "Frank went to Dr. Pinneo and was taught the rudiments of what he used to cure patients."
>
> **E. M. Bliss**

After learning all he could from Dr. Pinneo, under Anna's tutelage Frank gradually took over the care of most of the patients in Mosquito.

Some of these patients were those he had worked on while studying with Dr. Pinneo. Shortly thereafter Dr. Pinneo died and many of his patients followed Frank.

Neighbors first noticed patients coming to the cabin the last year the stagecoach ran from Placerville to Pino Grande, in 1924. The old stagecoach driver—Tom Simus (or Semas)—transported passengers, delivered mail and groceries, and let people off in Mosquito to visit the Goat Doctor and picked them up on his return trip the same day.

> "It was while working for a lumber company in Placerville that I learned about the Goat Doctor. Everybody there talked about him and said how effective he was. So, when I hurt my back, I went to him for treatment. I'll never forget the sight of him standing there barefoot in the midst of all those goats and chickens, in front of his cabin.
>
> "I was afraid of his mother. When she was instructing him, she spoke in short, abrupt, whip-like sentences. She was very strict with him. When she told him to do something, she wanted it done exactly her way. It seemed as though the minute she saw a person she knew what was wrong with them."
>
> **G. Parnell,** Reflexologist

"In the beginning Frank was apprentice to Anna's work and helped her with the patients. Later as Anna grew older, it was the other way around."

O. Beckett

Anna was happy to have Frank take over most of the treatments as it gave her some free time to do things she enjoyed such as riding her horse and roaming the hills searching for wild herbs and medicinal plants.

"We lived near the Andrés for eleven years. Anna was an herbalist and she and Frank did a lot of walking and looking for herbs. They were always using food that nature provided. I remember seeing her gathering pine nuts—they are so small—for food.

"My mother used to have treatments for her back. While waiting for her, I remember watching kids playing in the mud by the garden.

"When Frank was through treating her, he invariably said to me and my three siblings, 'Well, come and let me see about you.' He checked us often. He cared about us children."

C. Neilsen

"Anna liked to ride her horse all over the country and she would often ride to our house. My mother and Anna became good friends and we three would even have picnics together. One day, I should have been paddled; Anna said to my mother that she noticed how very observant I was. Actually, I was watching Annie's false teeth slipping up and down!"

L. Beckett-Pearson

"Anna wore long skirts. She had very dark piercing eyes and a large goiter, which made her eyes protrude. She was very scary to me as a child.

"One time, when she was in her fifties, a mean steer came at her while she was riding and she jumped off her horse, ran to the stile, leaped over the fence like a sixteen-year old, and got away". **L. Croft**

———————————

Frank and Anna never charged for their healings, yet people always wanted to give them something to express their gratitude. When asked, "What do I owe?" the usual answer was, "There is no charge, but if you would like, you can leave a donation in the container by the door."

If a person seemed unsure as to how much to give, they would sometimes mention the amount most people left or they would say something like, "Whatever you think it's worth."

Frank did not like to discuss money. Even suggesting an amount embarrassed him and often as not when the subject of money came up, he would go about his work pretending he did not hear.

Donations were not always in the form of money. People gave all sorts of things.

"It was in the mid 20's when, as a teenager, my dad injured his back when his car rolled over. He went to the Goat Doctor for help.

"The Goat Doctor worked on him while wearing only a loincloth. The room was barren except for the treatment table and an orange crate. The table was two saw horses with boards across them, covered with goatskins. The orange crate was for people to drop their donations through the slats and into the box.

"My father was a carpenter's apprentice and didn't have any money to give. So instead, because the Goat Doctor didn't have a decent treatment table, my father built him one." **B. Ryan**

"My dad, who was a teenager at the time, and my grandmother had just moved to Sacramento from Texas. He got a job driving a truck from Sacramento to Placerville. One day my dad threw his back out. He lay in the shack for many days in extreme pain, unable to get up.

"They were very poor, living in a three-sided shack. The wind would blow on him while he lay there. My grandmother had heard about the Goat Doctor. My dad had no choice. He had to do something. So, my grandmother and her friend took my dad to see the Goat Doctor.

"When they arrived, there was a line of people waiting. When it was his turn, he was brought in and laid upon a table.

"Unfortunately, my dad never told us exactly what the Goat Doctor did to him. Although, he had to be carried in, when the doctor was through with him, my dad walked out.

"My Dad had suffered from a bad back all of his life, but for all the years after his experience with the Goat Doctor, he was fine.

"The price for this healing—a couple of chickens."

G. Williams

"Ours was a large and active family with six children. Whenever someone had a bone out of place, we would head for the Goat Doctor. There would usually be a dozen or more cars already there.

"He always greeted us with a big smile. He always knew before anyone told him what had happened and why we were there. He always took care of our problem and money was never mentioned.

"He appreciated our bringing him walnuts or rabbits, and seemed especially pleased when we would drop off some butchered pork."   **C. Gemmet**

"We visited with a man who told us the Goat Doctor had treated him the week prior and would not accept money because he was unemployed. He said the family was surviving on monies from pies his wife baked and sold—made from apples off their own trees. The fellow waited for hours, holding a pie, anxious and happy to be able to show his gratitude."

C. Curtis

Ernest, yet living and working in San Francisco managed to keep busy. His poems and short stories were now in print in magazines and local newspapers, including the San Francisco Chronicle. Although most of his poems were cheerful, witty, and romantic, he could be bitingly critical when the subject had to do with current and historical affairs.

One day, he read about a science professor who while hunting for toads in his neighbor's yard, was mistaken for a prowling burglar and arrested. He was released by the police with a warning to advertise his future toad hunts by whistling or singing while hot on the trail of his prey.

Ernest could not resist responding to the article in jest and sent the newspaper this verse:

I'm a-Lookin' for Toads

I'm a-lookin' for toads, yes, a-lookin' for toads.
I finds 'em a-hoppin' all over the roads,
So I whistle and sing, It's a very strange thing,
That a man should be hindered from lookin' for toads.

I'm a-lookin' for toads, and I know their abodes.
And would you believe it, they all have their codes.

As I whistle and sing, they sit 'round in a ring,
Just a-croakin' in chorus: "He's lookin' for toads."

Now for beauty they never have taken a prize,
Though a jewel you'll find if you look in their eyes.
We find 'em illustrious in fables and odes —
But whistle and sing when you're lookin' for toads.

San Francisco Daily News -- 1927

The beginning of 1929 was a happy time for the André family. After twenty-some odd years of working for the plumbing company, Ernest retired and joined Anna and Frank in Mosquito.

He seemed to fit right in with Frank and Anna's unorthodox ways. Enjoying the freedom of not having to shave, he let his white hair and beard grow long. Then one a hot summer day, dressed in shorts (rarely worn by men there-about at the time), went for a walk on the land he had worked so hard and long to acquire.

> "I was walking along the road between our house and where the Andrés lived. I saw this half-naked man with white hair and white beard.
>
> "He was barefoot, wearing shorts and carrying a crooked walking stick. I was nearly scared to death! I ran home and told my mother, "I JUST SAW A WILD MAN!" It turned out to be Mr. André."
>
> **L. Beckett-Pearson**

The Andrés may have been Mosquito's most eccentric family, but they were also, three of the most intelligent people in the area. Ernest Francis André was born in London, England, on May 21, 1865. The son of Emma and

Nathaniel André and a direct descendant, of Major John André, the spy who was hanged during the Revolutionary War for collaborating with Benedict Arnold. "He was on the wrong side," Ernest said, "but it's an interesting fact."

For a number of years, Ernest was a student in various boarding schools in England and furthered his education by extensive travel and reading.

Young Ernest

After disembarking in New York in 1882, he held a variety of jobs while traveling across the country. At one point, he worked as a mule driver on the Erie Canal project. By 1893, he had worked his way to California.

After an unsuccessful attempt at mining for gold on the Mokelumne River in 1902, a flip of a coin decided his direction and he went to San Jose. There he met Anna Raker and they were married in 1906. It was Ernest's first marriage and Anna's second. [Shwartz is thought to be Anna's first husband's name.]

Ernest liked to refer to himself as a poet and a soldier of fortune. His hobby was etymology, the origin and development of words.

"I remember the first time we met Ernest. We had come up to see the land we had bought. It was the first time we had walked it.

"He was up on a hill sitting on a rock transcribing his shorthand notes on poetry. He would write the poems at night and rewrite them in the daytime while watching the goats.

"He was typically English with an English accent. Not a large man, not a dude, but was presentable."

V. Alexander

"Ernest was highly educated, a brilliant man."

E. M. Bliss

"Ernest was quiet, but extremely witty with a dry humor. He was about five-foot seven-inches tall, but appeared shorter because he walked very-stooped. He was of slight build and maybe one hundred forty to one hundred fifty pounds.

"He wore waist trousers and low cut shoes—ankle height. He displayed a real good intelligence. In our conversations, I gathered he was a bookkeeper.

"Because Dad André always had trouble with his bowels, Frank insisted that Ernest help herd the goats to get exercise.

"He'd turn the goats out early in the morning. They'd take off in groups with the old man following. In the afternoon, they'd start drifting back. I never saw Ernest do any other chores.

"When Dad André would herd the goats, he always carried a single-shot 22 rifle. He carried it by the muzzle and used it for a cane.

"That's a fact. The butt of that rifle was worn off like you couldn't believe. He had told me of killing gray squirrels to eat. I would imagine he also carried it to shoot coyotes because he spent a lot of time with the goats." **O. Beckett**

"I met Ernest when I was six years of age. I remember his blue-blue eyes and his marvelous sense of humor." **C. Neilsen**

"Ernest was a real character. He smoked a lot and somehow the smoke always came right at you. If he didn't like you, he just wouldn't even look at you."

A. Boeding

"We would sit out and talk with Ernest. He always had a hat on. He couldn't understand why they named cars. I was in his bedroom once. He had a 30-30 rifle, a cot, an orange crate, a clock, and a lamp."　　**M. Coburn**

"When I went down there and met Ernest, I found out he was a real fine old gentleman and was well educated and well read.

"He was also very hard of hearing. He told me one real good thing about being deaf or hard of hearing was nobody bothered to holler the bad things at him. I guess the good things were all he ever heard."

L. Beckett-Pearson

Shortly after moving to Mosquito Ernest took a part-time position with the American River Electric Company. His main job was that of a ditch tender. Anna often accompanied him as he made his inspections, walking alongside the flumes near the river, making sure they were free of debris.

Anna picked flowers and herbs along the way and Ernest stopped occasionally to jot down a line or two of a verse as they came to him, on his note pad. Many of his poetic inspirations came from his treks through the backcountry. His most popular and well remembered poem is about Mosquito Creek.

THE SONG OF MOSQUITO CREEK

In the morning gray as I wend my way
my wandering flock to seek
I tarry awhile by the dim defile
for the song of Mosquito Creek.

O it sings all night and it sings all day,
and it sings both high and low,
with a jubilant song as it journeys along
to a tryst with the river below.

It hails this bend as a well-known friend
as it ripples o'er granite and sand
Where the stately pine and the wild grape vine
unite in a brotherly band.

And it merrily glides where the turtle hides
and the bull-frogs serenade
By the darkened pool, serene and cool,
that sleeps in the cedar's shade.

And I hear it rejoice with a vibrant voice
as it runs by the rain-drenched fields.
In the fair spring time when the sweet wild thyme
Its spicy fragrance yields.

And it loudly calls as it rides the falls
where the oaks and the alders blend;
And it dashes away in a cloud of spray-
then on to its journey's end.

It murmurs low of the long ago
before the white man came,
When the Indian carried his trusty bow
and hunted his chosen game.

And saw no sign of a coming time
when a ruthless, alien race
Would narrow the bounds of his hunting grounds
and trade in his soul's disgrace.

And it sings again with a gay refrain
of the days of Auld Lang Syne
When Fortune's wiles drew tears and smiles
From her suitors in Forty-Nine.

When many gained wealth and some gained health
and a few enduring names;
But many more slept where the shadows crept
over ruined and barren claims.

On these rude stones, embossed with cones,
Where a wren has reared her nest,
A cabin once stood in the sheltering wood –
but the builder has gone to his rest.

And, a prey to the rains, I see the remains
of the rocker he used of old;
But the hand that panned the gravel and sand
no longer uncover the gold.

Near this ravine, where the grass is green,
were the diggin's of old Tom Moore,
Who always ate when the table was set,
but seldom paid his score.

And on this grade, in the bountiful shade
of a spreading live oak tree,
They held a wake over New York Jake,
at the end of a fatal spree.

Oh! This stuttering creek if it only could speak
what tales it could tell us of yore
But the smiles and the tears have gone with the years
and the clamor is heard no more.

Now grazing cattle and browsing goats,
and at times a startled deer,
Have taken 'the place of the sturdy race
that struggled for fortune here.

And as I dream by the friendly stream
and ponder on men and things.
I fancy I hear a message of cheer
and hope as It joyously sings.

And still it will sing in winter and spring,
as it rides the canyon's side,
When you and I and the passersby
 are over the Great Divide!

Ernest André

Within months of Ernest's retirement, a tragedy marred the Andrés' happy reunion. The men were gone when Anna and Ernest's house caught fire and burned to the ground. Some people speculated the fire started in the kitchen closet that

Frank had converted into a dark room for his hobby of photography.

"I remember as a child I watched Frank André develop his own snapshots in a closet in the kitchen. I was 13 years of age when their first house burned down in June of 1929. Anna hurt her back real bad struggling to get the treatment table out. It was heavy as lead. They never knew for sure what caused the fire."   **L. Beckett-Pearson**

"Ann was left semi-crippled trying to get that big table out of the house. It was the only thing saved from the fire."   **Lois Croft**

———————

Everything changed after the fire. The one room cabin now served as the Andrés' home as well as Frank's treatment room.

A large drape, made of goatskins sewn together, hung from wall to wall in the middle of the room separating the family's private living quarters in the back and the treatment area in front.

Centered, in front of the drape, was the heavy hand-hewn table Anna saved from the fire. It was four feet wide by eight feet in length, counter height and had a movable contoured wooden pillow. Next to this table, on the left side of the room was a three-foot by six-foot slightly lower table. This table was mainly for patients to lie upon with hot water bottles to relax their muscles before adjustments.

Behind the drape were a small table and some chairs in front of the fireplace. The drape closed at the foot of Frank's bed (now used by Anna), safely beyond a wood-burning kitchen stove on the right wall. Ernest slept on the treatment table, while Frank either slept in the barn or camped out.

"I used to see him in the far off distance in his loincloth, herding his goats. This was not long after his parents moved into the cabin. After he had taken the goats high up in the hills to graze, he would go to the cabin, clean up, put on a clean shirt and bib overalls before treating patients.

"He had high cheek bones and was real handsome." **D. Cupps**

"I first met the Goat Doctor, he was always Frank to me, shortly after his parents' house burned down. I was mining at Sweetwater Creek. I must have crossed that old trestle bridge a hundred times.

"He was camping alone in the mountains, eating wild berries, drinking goat's milk, and sleeping in a little tent." **W. Durfey**

Wil Durfey and friend

Friends and patients brought seeds and plants of every kind of vegetable and herb imaginable for two new gardens.

One garden, in front and to the left of the cabin door, extended approximately twenty feet forward on fairly - level ground, before continuing off to the left. It followed the downward grade of the land, growing around rocks that made up much of the rugged terrain.

Behind this garden, descending a steep hill was an orchard of apple, cherry, lemon, orange, pear, and nut trees. These grew among the alder, bay, cedar, oak, pine, poplar, willow trees, and manzanita that grew all about the property.

On the right side of the path that led to the cabin door, another garden extended forward from the cabin and followed the curvature atop the bank of the ravine.

Some of the herbs in this garden (many still growing there today) are bear clover, blessed thistle, chamomile, chickweed, and cleavers. There was also dandelion, fennel, horehound, horsemint and horsetail, as well as lemon balm, malva, mountain misery and mugwart.

One could find mullein, nettle, plantain, scotch-broom, and Shepard's purse, along with St. John's wort, star thistle, wild oats, wild lettuce, yellow dock, and thick patches of wild black berries. There were roses, sunflowers, marigolds, and wild daisies growing in and around both gardens. Through the years, they added lilacs, irises, and daffodils.

Every conceivable type of board, post, or wood remnant; along with tree branches and chicken wire were used to build fences around the gardens that covered close to half an acre.

"He had a large vegetable garden and everything in it was **extra** big. I remember the place as very clean with beautiful roses and huge sunflowers growing in the front yard." **D. Pederson**

The old barn that housed the goats, already inadequate in size, was now inconvenient in location. The men chopped, stripped, and split logs to build a new twenty by forty-foot barn adjacent to the county road and closer to the cabin.

Built on a slope, the working barn had two levels. It included stalls, a tack room, and a hayloft. In the upper level, where the nannies were stalled; a section of the floor was spaced so that manure could be raked through the opening and fall to the ground, making it easier to remove.

Two-thirds of the lower section was used to house the bucks, a mule or two and for storage.

The goat barn

"My brothers had a sawmill and Frank bought lumber from them. He was getting fifty cents a treatment and paid my brother with four-bit pieces."

E. M. Bliss

The dray wagon was moved behind and a little to the left of the goat barn. The canned foods, blankets, and other supplies stocked in the wagon, helped sustain them through this difficult period.

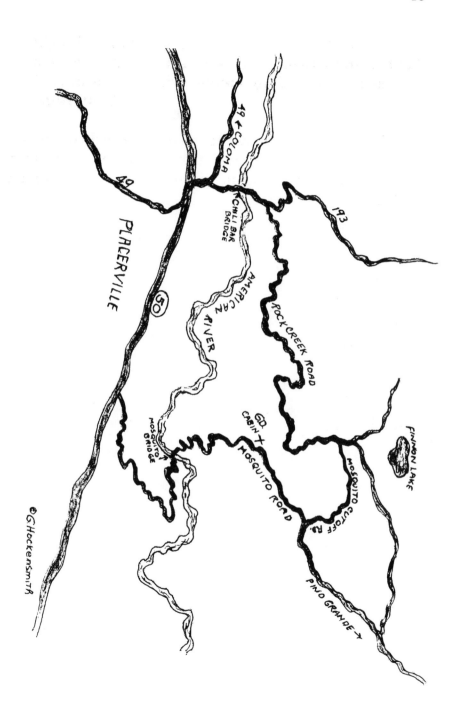

44

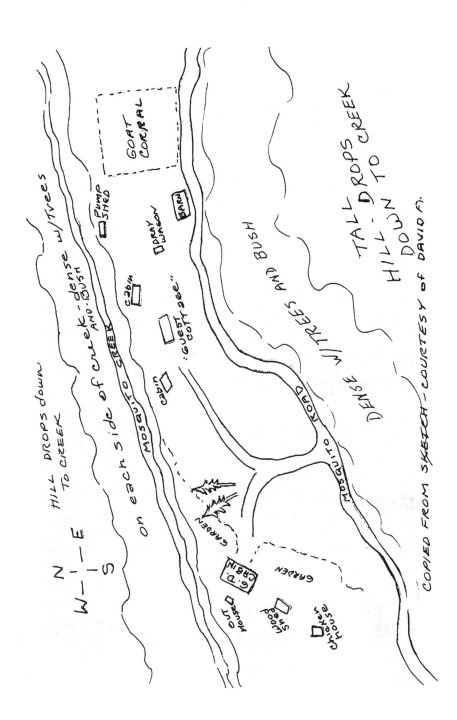

COPIED FROM SKETCH - COURTESY OF DAVID F.

Chapter Three
1930 – 1939

Frank André

In the early thirties, Frank became aware of names called him by the local gossips. He knew he had been dubbed "Goat Doctor" as a derogatory pun but this he never really minded as he felt the goats had virtually saved his life. However, he became so upset when he heard people were calling him "The Nature Faker," a "Charlatan," and a "Quack," he decided he would go to a Chiropractic College and get a degree.

"Frank was a sensitive man. He was terribly hurt by the degrading remarks that had gotten back to him. Our whole family thought the world of Frank André. I remember how 'up in arms' we'd get whenever we heard something said about him that was not true.

"Even though he and Anna had complete confidence in his procedures and abilities, it became very important to Frank that he receive a chiropractic diploma. He wanted it for one reason only—to hang it on the wall in his treatment room. He wanted the respect that came with it.

"I can remember the time he went away to college. My mother was really suffering from back pain while he was gone. She went around the house bemoaning the fact that Frank wasn't there to give her a treatment. Several months later, he came home, but without a license."   **C. Neilsen**

"Frank went to school in southern California for about six to eight months. He got into several arguments with the instructors on how to treat patients and quit."   **G. Ainsleigh, D.C.**

———————

Frank returned to Mosquito a very sad and disheartened man, but had little time to dwell on his upset as word spread fast that he was back and his days became filled with patients. It was also at this time (1933) that he met and became friends with a new neighbor—Orval Beckett.

Lois and Orval Beckett

"When I first heard of him, it sounded like he was a spiritual leader. Depending on who you were talking with, this was good or bad. One person would go on about that 'kook' down the road and his mother and their cult of devil worshippers.

"Another person would go on about the wonderful faith healer and family who did so much good.

"Not long after moving to Mosquito and finding work, I injured my back in a fall. We had a washout down on the American River flumes. We'd work long hours. The boss said it was quitting time.

"I started to throw a rock, but it was a little too heavy for a person to be lifting, and down I went. My employer, PG&E, didn't recognize chiropractors, but the boss foreman did. He lived about a quarter mile from the Andrés. Les was our superintendent. He was a 'great big man', about 5'3", weighing about 110 pounds soaked in oil.

"'Well, what do you want to do, go to the hospital or to the Goat Doctor?' he asked. By this time I'd heard the men at work telling how good he was at fixing up people, so I answered, 'The Goat Doctor!'

"One of the men who helped to get me there asked the foreman, 'Do you want us to stay?'

"'Heck no,' Les said, 'After he sees the Goat Doctor he can walk home!' Sure enough, the doc twisted me a couple of times and I got up and walked out.

"After that, I spent a lot of time at his place. I found Frank André to be a very nice gentleman who appeared to be formally educated.

"Frank treated me and I did odd jobs for him in trade. I used to clean the goat shed out with Lysol. I helped with the shearing and butchering of the goats.

"There were cement troughs next to the barn and twice a year we would dip the goats. Some of the billys were too big for Frank to do alone, so I'd help him. When we got through, we looked more like a goat than the goats did! Probably smelled like a goat, too!

"When we'd be dipping the goats, the gentle ones, Frank would have me feel their spines and explain to me how each segment went to a certain organ.

"I did a lot of carpentry work, and chopped and piled his yearly supply of wood. My wife and I hauled lots of groceries out to him, from town.

"I used to lift people out of their cars and carry people down the hill to the cabin, as most of them couldn't make it on their own when they first got there. They'd be in there a few minutes and come out walking.

"He kept up-to-date on new medicines and when someone asked him about a certain one, although he never prescribed any, he would tell them what he thought about it.

"Frank was a very gifted person. He and his mother worked together real closely. I heard of instances when he didn't know what to do. I saw him leave a patient on the table for maybe 10 to 15 minutes, go in the other room, consult his mother, and take their particular problem to the Lord in prayer."   **O. Beckett**

No one told of the Andrés attending church in Mosquito, however they were known to be a religious family. Anna and Ernest had belonged to the Rosicrucian Society while living in San Jose.

Below is copied from the calling card Anna gave out in the 30's and forties. They used postcards that read the same.

DRS. F. M. and A. E. ANDRÉ

Intuitive Researchers and Demonstrators
of Natural and Spiritual Laws of Creation
Laws Veiled in Symbolism in the Scriptures
I. E. Bible Science

PLACERVILLE, CALIFORNIA
MOSQUITO DISTRICT

Many people interviewed told of Anna praying over someone after a healing treatment, and some mentioned Frank doing it also. Although, ten times as many people told how strongly they felt Frank André resembled the pictures they had seen that personified Jesus, and how he exuded an aura of spirituality.

"I remember the first time I saw him. We were driving our Model-T up the American River Canyon Road. Down the road comes this barefooted guy with long hair and a herd of goats. I thought he was Jesus Christ. That was my first impression of him."
D. Arsenith – P. Presba - Georgetown Gazette

"It was strange. He never preached religion or even spoke of it, yet he radiated a special spiritual feeling." **J. Roberts**

"I was just a child, but my first thought on meeting him was I just met God. There was such a strong spiritualistic feeling around him when in his presence." **P. Moore**

"Frank lived his religion every day—it was just his way of life." **D. Dodge**

"It's hard to describe, but the man had a streak of religion in him and gave people spiritual help."
F. Fausell

"Ours was not an actively or overly religious family, but one and all agreed, after seeing the Goat Doctor, he seemed to have a Christ-like aura about him." **G. Hopkins**

"When I looked into his eyes, I felt I was looking into the eyes of Jesus." **D. Madigan**

"André had a beard and the most beautiful dark eyes. He had really nice features. I was so impressed with his looks and I remember saying to my mother he had a Christ-like appearance." **S. Hill**

"He trusted in the Lord and when he wasn't sure about treating someone, he would go in the next room and pray." **D. Pederson**

"He was a naturalist and lived off the land. He did hands-on healing type of work. My five-year-old brother had just started Bible school. One day he saw Frank going into the old Purity Market. He asked our mother if that was Jesus." **A. Ginelle**

"It was like being in the presence of Jesus—his eyes were almost hypnotic." **L. Loudon**

"About every month or so on our way home from Placerville to Pino Grande, my parents would stop in Mosquito. My father used to buy goat meat from Frank and my mother would buy vegetables from Mrs. André.
"I never saw Frank wearing shoes, only sandals. I remember his beautiful long hair. He wore it in a thick braid with the end tucked in under his belt. I always told my mother he looked just like Jesus." **L. Croft**

"The thing that comes to my mind first about Frank André is how much he resembled the pictures of Christ you always see. He was very soft spoken and kind. I recall him smiling a lot and his gentle eyes. As a child, I thought he was the greatest thing next to ice cream." **J. Dixon**

"We lived near the Andrés for years. When I first met him he had a full beard, his hair, which appeared to have never been cut, was tied back in a ponytail with a black ribbon, and he looked just like the pictures of Christ—identical—you could not have told the difference. At the same time, he appeared to be the strongest man I had ever known."   **C. Neilsen**

"Frank had such quiet, soft manners. He had real pretty brown eyes and was a very handsome and kind man.

"He was often compared with pictures of Christ. I knew him better then anyone and I felt he had that appearance."   **L. Beckett-Pearson**

"When we met the Goat Doctor the first thing we noticed was his personality. Most of all his great big smile—and he always used it!

"Besides his smile, you couldn't help but notice his hair. It was a real attention-getter. He sometimes wore it braided or tied, hanging down to the middle of his back. He appeared to have never had a haircut!

"One day a 16-year old high school girl who lived nearby wanted to meet Frank. She knew we knew him. She asked us to have him over to our house to meet him. She raved from then on, about how beautiful he was and how he looked just like God. Of course, she meant Jesus.

"I had a problem with my sacroiliac, so I went to see Frank. First, he had me lie on my back on the table. Then he had me lie on my side.

"He said, 'You have two problems in the lower pelvic area, one being the cartilage holding the hip joint flips back and forth.'

"He didn't do a massage. He just moved me a little and had me double up my leg. Then, he pulled my leg out and away from the table and rotated it. He fixed me up just fine!

"He said, 'If people walked more than they rode they wouldn't have this kind of problem!'"

B. Alexander

Frank told the majority of his patients with back problems to take walks as a simple exercise. He enjoyed walking and every now and again was seen walking into Placerville with several goats tagging behind.

When motorists stopped to offer him a ride, he usually refused. Not only, because he enjoyed walking, but because doctors had warned him gas fumes were dangerous to his remaining lung.

"I had a female friend who was crippled and confined to a wheelchair. The Goat Doctor said she would need on-going treatment, once a week for three months. He let me drive him to Georgetown, although I could tell he didn't like going in a car. When he finished treating her, she walked again.

"Frank told me how he used to sleep with his goats, claiming powers from goat oil." **J. VonBulow**

"He had such a fear of gas fumes. One day, a man I knew in Placerville had such pain he just couldn't stand to get in a car for the ride out to Mosquito. I drove clear out to Frank's place to bring Frank to the man.

"Frank hemmed and hawed for a couple of minutes. He did not like the idea of going in the car because of the fumes, but he went. The man had a pinched-vertebra that had paralyzed his leg. Frank fixed him up just fine." **E. Teany**

"We knew the Andrés from the time they moved to Mosquito.   Although Frank seldom rode in an automobile, because he said, the fumes from the car were dangerous and he only had one lung. He let my brother-in-law drive him to the house where my sister lay bedridden with a bad back.

"Frank put her on the ironing board and put her back, back in place. He also worked on my neck and I've never had any trouble since.

"He would not work on my brother. He said he could do him no good. I think Frank knew he had cancer."   **E. M. Bliss**

"The doctor told me about a day when he had a bad tooth, and was walking into Placerville to have it pulled. He had walked about seven miles when a car pulled up and asked if he could tell them how to get to the Goat Doctor's place.

"These people said they were from Idaho and that they needed him. He said he just couldn't turn them down. As bad as he felt and as much as he didn't like riding in cars, he went back to the cabin with them to give a treatment."   **H. Rominger**

Where Anna knew a patient's condition just by looking at them, Frank had to touch a person. He was then intuitive in the respect that not only did he sense their problem, he was able to tell how and when an injury occurred. Patients were never required to remove clothing.

"After some gentle manipulating on my back, he told me I should not have had the surgery I'd had done, as it had only worsened my condition. He worked for a while longer then said the surgery had done more harm than good. This was amazing in the

fact that he did not have me disrobe and I had not
mentioned having had surgery." **F. Matzka**

"It was unreal. He could just touch people, tell
them what was wrong, and heal them." **L. Loudon**

"Frank was unbelievable. You did not have to tell
him where you hurt, or how you were injured—he
already knew!" **J.D. Lawson**

"I went to him many times. He never had me
disrobe. I asked him why and he said it wasn't at all
necessary." **I. Radonich**

"Other than shoes, he never had people take
clothing off, except maybe a heavy overcoat or a big
belt." **A. Boeding**

"One day I told my father that I was going to take
my fiancé out to see Dr. André. My father said, 'You'd
better get there early.' I believe it was Memorial Day.
I didn't think it would be very busy, but we got there
around four in the morning. There were at least
fifteen cars ahead of us.
"My fiancé had a soreness in her lower back and
perpetual sniffles. This gal's parents were very
wealthy and they had taken her to every doctor they
had heard of, and she still had a sore back and
sniffles.
"I remember the Goat Doctor had huge hands. He
had her lay on the table, she did not have to remove
any clothing, and he measured her legs. Then he told
her how she had been injured as a child.
"He said the problems she had now had come from
that injury. He took her ankle and had her do a few
sit-ups. Then, told me I should help her with this

type of exercise for two months and then return to
him.

"When we returned, he did an adjustment and she
came out of his place yelling yah-hoo! She was fine
from then on. Even her sniffles were gone!"

R. Weichold

"The main thing I remember was he seemed to
know what was wrong with people before they told
him—even before he checked them over."

R. Randall

"He would not work if someone were talking in the
room. He would stop and stand perfectly erect. He
could tell people how and when they were hurt
without their saying a word.

"He wanted me to hear his favorite song. He went
into another room, wound up his Victrola, and played
'The Loveliest Night of the Year.'" **D. Madigan**

Whether it was intuition or he was attracted to them, a
few women told of Frank saying to them, "How come it took
you so long to get here, I've been waiting for you?"

———————

Anyone who experienced his psychic ability of knowing their
ailment without their telling him could not help but tell
others when recommending Frank to them. To see if he
could tell them what or where their ailment was, people
began testing him by keeping quiet.

"People used to deliberately not tell him where
their pain was. He always found their problem
immediately." **L. Kelley**

"I'd say I went up the first time to see him about 1932 or 1933. I was working out here on a Harvester Plainfield. I had what they called a leader cart.

"We were always having to replace a wheel on it. I would raise the cart and another guy would put the wheel on. But this time the guy walked right by, so I decided okay, what the heck, I'll just put the wheel on myself. I reached down, picked up the wheel, and put it on. That afternoon, I was on the tractor and could feel there was a little pain in my shoulder. It wasn't too bad.

"By that night, I was doubled-up in pain, it hurt so bad. So, I went to the Woodland Clinic and they worked on my back. It didn't do any good.

"My sister had heard of the Goat Doctor and suggested I go see him. Well, my brother took me there and I got in his workroom and started to take my shirt off.

"'Oh, you don't have to take your shirt off,' he said. I thought 'what the- Sam-heck?'

"He had me lay down all stretched out on a big old table. I'd heard about how he was supposed to know what was wrong without anyone telling him and I wanted to see if he could, so I just kept quiet.

"He sat on a stool behind me and felt my neck first, and then he got up and had me roll over. He started walking around me feeling up and down my back. He touched where it hurt, but I thought, 'So help me, I am not going to let him know where'.

"I didn't make a sound. He stopped and talked for a while with my brother about farming and how dangerous the chemicals in fertilizers were.

"Then he started to knead my neck a little, then went to my back again right over the sore spot where the pressure and pain was. He worked on that spot a bit then told me to put a hot water bottle on it for a while when I got home. Only in real bad cases did he ever want to see you again.

"'You might be a little sore,' he told me.

"I thought, 'how could I be sore—he didn't do anything to make me sore or that did any good'.

"He explained to me how vertebrae get pinched and that was what caused the problem. Every bone would snap and he could do it so easily, no pain or anything. He was strong—he used to grab me by my butt and move me.

"Dr. André said all those diathermy lights did was draw the inflammation up and relieve the pain, not correct it, and it would come back again.

"I asked how much I owed and he didn't say anything, so I just gave him a couple of dollars or so.

"By the time I got home, I realized the pain was gone. He fixed me up in that one treatment."

H. Rominger

When asked how he could possibly know a person's predicament without being told, Frank's usual reply was it was "intuitive medicine" or "sixth sense".

"Another time, my wife and I went up there and he was butchering a goat. He had his boots on. I was curious as to how he could tell a person's problem so accurately after barely touching them, so I started asking him questions.

"'Well, you know,' he explained, as he pointed to his boots, 'it's like when you're putting on your boots and you miss one of the hooks when you lace it, you can feel down and find what hook you missed. Well, that's just the way I can feel it in your back.'

"I was kind of hard headed and wouldn't have ever believed a lot of that stuff if I hadn't seen it for myself."

H. Rominger

"I asked him what he called himself. He said he was an intuitive adjuster. He could just run his fingers along my spine and say, 'Oops, there it is!' It was just like pressing your finger on an abscessed tooth." **C. Otis**

"The question came up as to how he could possibly know a person's problem by barely touching them. 'Let me show you something,' he said. Then, he did something that I'll never forget.

"He pulled a hair out of the side of his head and handed it to me. He then handed me a Bible and told me to put the hair anywhere I wanted inside the Bible and to close it.

"He put one of his hands on top of the hard-covered book and barely felt it with his fingers before telling us the exact page it was on.

"We were amazed. He seemed to enjoy showing us and did this a couple more times." **W. Langton**

During this time-period—the great depression—bartering became common throughout the United States.

"I went to the Goat Doctor in the 30's when I had malaria. He always had you lay down on his table and he would stretch your legs to compare their length.

"He had me stay at his cabin for one week; this was when it was still a one-room cabin. He put me on a diet of lemon rind, raw carrots, and goat's milk.

"That's all I had to eat for a total of two weeks. I went into the service a few years later and was sent overseas. I was exposed to malaria but have never had a reoccurrence.

"He had one treatment table and under the treatment table were a couple of nests. There were at least six chicken nests in that room. One nest sat on top of a milk bucket that was filled with silver dollars.

"Their main livelihood came from their animals. They did a lot of bartering, even trading for 80-pound sacks of flour. I used to pick up big sacks of chicken grain for him."   **A. Boeding**

"Everybody around here knew the Goat Doctor and went to him for their health. Times were hard and a lot of trading went on in helping one another.

"So, instead of money, the neighbors did chores for Frank in trade for his taking care of them and their families. Some even helped him with building rooms onto his cabin.

"I could never have worked most of my years except for Frank, so I put in a lot of time at his place.

"One day there, my wife and I talked with a man who said he'd been on crutches for 17 years. We watched him go into Frank's treatment room, then saw him come out walking. His face was wet with tears."   **W. Alexander**

After sharing the one room cabin for approximately six years, in 1935, with the help of patients and friends, Frank built an addition onto the cabin.

On the right wall the length of the cabin, leaving the windows intact, they built a kitchen approximately eight-feet wide. The inside and outside walls were one-and-the-same, rough-sawn, unpainted timber with slats covering the cracks. A door from the treatment room led to the kitchen.

They moved the kitchen stove between two windows along the new right wall. A kitchen sink was installed left of the stove and beyond the sink an outside door opened onto a small porch. Stairs from the porch led to a narrow patch of earth along the crest of the ravine and Mosquito Creek.

A few months later, a bedroom was built for Ernest and Anna behind part of the treatment room and kitchen. You entered the bedroom through the back door of the treatment room and a door on the left wall of the bedroom opened out to a new porch and staircase to the ground.

Using the high ceiling space of the A-frame cabin, they nailed wood to the joists to make a floor. This loft became Frank's bedroom. Steep stairs led to the loft from behind the goatskin drape in the treatment room.

The Andrés now ate their meals at a small table in the kitchen. When they had company, they pulled the drape aside and the treatment room became their dining room.

> "The Goat Doctor would take the goat hides off the treatment table and put on a tablecloth. Many people from my church, also patients, took meals with him."
> **H. Bigelo**

Around the fireplace—which no one could recall ever seeing a fire in—Frank built an extra large hearth out of cement. There was no electricity, only lanterns and candles for light and kerosene heaters and woodstoves for heat.

> "I remember Frank telling me they had no electricity because he was afraid it would cause a fire."
> **P. DeWolfe**

With the exception of the back bedroom, the wood floors were surfaced with linoleum and goat hides covered most of the floors.

> "He had goatskins all over the floors. I used to love to go over to his place and I remember lying down on them and petting them."
> **J. Dixon**

"I remember the goatskin rugs all over the floors and asking if I could touch them. We were raised very proper and you asked before you touched anything that belonged to someone else. I remember thinking, what a wonderful feeling, and how I'd never felt anything so very, very soft."   **D. Montgomery**

"The Angora goatskins felt so good to bare feet. The skins were never tanned, they just let them dry out, and when you walked on them, they always made a crackling noise."   **C. Neilsen**

When Orval was laid-off work in the late thirties, Frank hired him to build a screened-in waiting room onto the front of the treatment room. Patients now entered the treatment area through the waiting room.

The room was approximately eight feet deep and sixteen feet wide. It contained a few of Frank's handmade chairs and orange crates for seating. The orange-crates were eventually replaced with three long pew-like benches.

There was a hole in the wall for chickens to come and go, and boxes with straw were under the benches for chickens to roost. New patients were always surprised at the obvious difference between Frank's working environment and a typical doctor's office.

"It was quite unusual inside the cabin, very dark, no lights—only a couple of tiny windows in his treatment room. It was eerie, really-spooky."   **B. Webster**

"We waited our turn in a porch-like area. We barely got situated on one of the three pew-like benches when we heard a rustling sound under the bench we were seated on.

"I bent down to see what was going on. My eyes were met by a pair of bright, piercing, beady eyes of a very indignant chicken who seemed to be just as curious as to what was going on above. It was really hilarious!"   **D. Cupps**

"The Goat Doctor worked on my father. I took my dad there twice and well, it sure didn't look like a doctor's office."   **R. Randall**

"Not only were there goatskins on the treatment table, every now and then a live goat had to be shooed off of it."   **T. Rulison, M.D.**

"It was eight a.m. when a woman opened the front door of the cabin and asked the first people to come into a screened-in porch.

"When our turn came, after making our way past a few goats, cats, dogs and peacocks, we found the waiting room for people doubled as a laying room for chickens!

"Every now and then, as the urgency arose, a hen would come running through a hole in the wall, hop in a box, let out a cackle, and lay an egg or visa versa!"   **C. Curtis**

"Chickens and goats were coming and going as we waited in the screened-in porch. One chicken paid no attention to us as it went about its business of hopping in a box to lay an egg.

"A goat wandered in, checked out my fingers and decided my ring would make a nice nibbly. I had to let him know differently."   **F. Matzka**

"There was a white rooster. It used to stand at the front of the house and attack people!"   **T. Sigwart**

"The animals had free run of the waiting room. While I sat there, a goat wandered in leaving his droppings on the porch as he left."   **H. Brown**

"The Andrés were definitely free-spirited. Chickens were nesting all over the place."   **M. Avery**

"A chicken came in and laid her egg in her favorite spot. Four people waiting their turn to see the Goat Doctor evidently had been there before because they paid little attention to the barnyard atmosphere of the waiting room."   **A. Williams**

"I remember well the chickens in the room, where people waited, and the goats all over the place. But people loved him and the way he lived didn't stop anybody from going there."   **T. Neeley**

"This kind of appearance would not seem to instill confidence but his practice grew and grew until he was working seven long days a week."
          P. Presba - Georgetown Gazette

The following year Orval built a separate bedroom for Anna adjacent to the waiting room. Three doors opened into Anna's room: a door for the family to enter the house from outside, a door from the waiting room, and a door from the kitchen.

The cabin's old wood roof was covered-over with the same corrugated metal as used on the new rooms. They built awnings on-to the two rooms in front of the cabin, to give protection to people waiting out-of-doors. Benches were made of orange crates with boards atop of them.

Goat Doctor/patients (a few years later) Courtesy of E. Kamp

Frank and Orval placed a gas powered pump near the edge of Mosquito Creek and piped water through the kitchen's wood-burning stove to the sink. No longer did they have to heat kettles of water for the hot water bottles and hot compresses.

A nearby spring provided water for years, but it was sparse at times and now used only for drinking and cooking.

"During the time I waited, I noticed his kitchen sink faucet had a stream of water running from it. In talking with Dr. Andre I learned he had piped the water from a nearby spring to bring the water into the house and that it had run that way for years! He said, 'Spring-water is much healthier than any water served in a fine restaurant.'"   **L. Oakes**

In 1937, after four years of construction, the Civilian Conservation Corps completed Rock Creek Road.

View from high atop Rock Creek Road of American River and Rock Creek Road

There were now two roads leading into Mosquito.

Mosquito Bridge was re-built the same year. Although still only one lane: railings were added, new wood trusses replaced the old, and new cables were anchored in cement pillars. A large boulder was cut back to make the turn onto the bridge easier.

With the new road and improved bridge, many more people made their way to Mosquito Canyon.

"Mosquito has always been just a settlement. The nearest grocery store was in Placerville. To go or come from town for anything we had to go past the André's place. For years, it was hard for all the neighbors to get through the traffic of cars. After they built Rock Creek Road, it was next to impossible. That's the way it was, day in and day out. I don't know how so many people heard of him."

L. Beckett-Pearson

"We know for a fact that from 1937 on, there were always cars out in front of his place. Sometimes they were squeezed in on both sides of the road for a mile or more!

"At this time, the doctor didn't have hours—he just took people 'til too tired. People brought blankets and food, and just plain camped out until he saw them!

"Only once did I ever see Frank get annoyed with people. He heard someone arguing as to who was next. He just said, 'that's all for today' and closed the door." **V. Alexander**

"By the late thirties, people were coming from Los Angeles and all over to Frank. You cannot imagine the multitude of cars that lined the road in front of his cabin.

"The Polio epidemic was at it's worst in the thirties and it was mainly the high school aged children who were crippled. I can't remember the girl's name, just that she was a county official's daughter.

"She was so badly crippled that it was all she could do to get around on crutches. Anyway, she told me that in spite of opposition, her parents took her to Frank and when telling me this, she was walking without any help." **E. M. Bliss**

"I worked for the Forest Service in the Mosquito area. I had to go past the Goat Doctor's place to get to work. It was not easy. The hunters and fishermen were always complaining because of all the cars lined up in front of his place. I got to know a lot of prospectors who went to him.

"I remember early on Frank telling me how he lived with the goats in the goat shed because the touch and the smell of them had a healing effect." **F. Fausell**

"We couldn't believe it—it was only six in the morning yet there were people everywhere. They were in and around cars, next to tents and huddled around campfires.

"The air was abuzz with chatter as the people visited with one another while anxiously waiting to see the Goat Doctor.

"Looking back towards the barn, we saw an old man followed by several goats making his way down a path that led to the cabin.

"A younger man came out of the cabin to greet him. He was barefoot and wore loose fitting denim overalls. He had a mustache, a goatee, and graying brown hair pulled back in a ponytail that hung well below the middle of his back! He fit the description given to us of the Goat Doctor!

"The chatter from the throngs of people ceased the moment he stepped out the cabin door; there was stone dead silence as.

"The two men exchanged a few words, then the older man continued to herd the goats around to the back of the cabin.

"The instant the Goat Doctor stepped back into the cabin the buzzing chatter returned all at once, as though someone had turned on a radio." **H. Brown**

"It was not uncommon to see cars lined up a mile and a half or more on Friday nights." **Dr. Craig**

"When our friend Bill's back went out I took him to see Frank who was now living in the cabin. If you didn't know him, it was a hard, long wait to see him We'd go in the back way and they'd take us right in.

"It was amazing the way he could twist old Bill around considering he weighed close to 300 pounds.

"The last time we went over to see Frank there were tents and people all over the hills. It was so damned crowded. Seemed like overnight there were people from everywhere coming to him.

"It was the darndest thing you ever saw. Frank was of the habit of stopping midday for one hour to eat and rest. There were literally hundreds of people all over the place waiting to see him and he would be in there sound asleep, taking a nap!" **W. Durfey**

A nap was no-doubt needed, especially after Frank had been called-upon to treat someone in the middle of the night.

"Myself and a couple of friends went out on the town, so to speak. During the course of the evening, this one fellow took up with this gal. Well, he was always cheating on his wife, but this night she came a looking for him.

"He was upstairs with a gal in a rented room when I saw the wife come in. I ran up there and told him. Damned if he didn't jump out the window!

"He hurt his ankles real bad. We were in town and it wasn't until after midnight by the time we got him over to the old Goat Doctor's place.

"We were all pretty pie-eyed so I don't remember what all he did other then he had us carry our friend down to the creek and stick his legs in the ice cold water.

"Anyway, whether he broke or sprained his ankles, I don't know, I just know he was right as rain within a day or two." **Anonymous**

"The first time I knew of him was when I was 16 or 17. A friend of mine had hurt his back real bad and had to work the next day. He was so bad off so we went there in the middle of a very black night.

"We got there shortly before midnight. We got Dr. André out of bed. It was not uncommon for people to come in the middle of the night, because he treated so many of the loggers.

"He didn't mind at all getting up at all hours of the night to help a person. He was always kind and gentle and never seemed to show any annoyance.

"His mother was there and she got up also and was of tremendous help. **D. Dodge**

A pyramid effect took over as one person told another about "The Miracle Worker." People were making their way to the cabin from all over the United States. Some made the trip once a year for their annual medical checkup; others formed groups and car-pooled to him, while some came just out of curiosity.

"On several occasions, my parents and I drove out to the shack where the Goat Doctor lived and treated people. It was all very primitive.

"I was always amazed at the cavalcade of vehicles along the road leading up to his place. There were older and smaller cars there, but I was especially fascinated to see so many big, shiny new cars, as they were incongruous to the area.

"All of the occupants of these vehicles were watching as this elderly man dawdled about doing his morning chores caring for his animals, seemingly oblivious to the mass of spectators watching his every move.

"We went there one time for some medical reason on my mother's behalf. I remember her saying there was a persona around him that was consuming and a sereneness about him that had a very calming effect on people. She referred to him as a very gentle man.

"One summer, relatives came for a visit. They had heard of the Goat Doctor in their hometown of Windover, Massachusetts and the Goat Doctor's place was on their agenda of tourist attractions."

S. Helmrich

"After my treatment, my husband and I, avid people-watchers, stayed a while longer and saw a very memorable event.

"We watched as two young men guided a wheel chair that carried a girl of about ten years of age, down the road to the path that led to the cabin.

"While the girl received treatment, the young men visited with us. They told us how their sister was crippled, six years prior, while skiing.

"Several specialists had seen her and their consensus had been unanimous—she would remain a cripple the rest of her life!

"After a neighbor told the girl's family what he had heard about the Goat Doctor in California, in a last desperate attempt to help her, the brothers had driven their sister all the way from Minnesota.

"Approximately 30 minutes later, the door opened and the doctor's helper beckoned the brothers to come in.

"Within minutes, the door opened again and the young girl appeared with her oldest brother at her side. She was smiling from ear to ear and yet crying at the same time.

"With one hand holding the girl's hand, the brother cupped his other hand under her arm to brace her. The Goat Doctor walked over to them and told him that was not at all necessary—she would be fine on her own.

"The brother released her and cautiously walked alongside of her as they made their way back up the hill. The other very red-eyed brother trailed behind pushing the wheelchair.

"As they drove away, no one made a sound, everybody there just stood staring into the space, where their car had been before disappearing around the curve."   **A. Anderson**

"We took the wife's sister up there one time. She just wanted to see the place.

"It was a rainy day so I didn't think there would be too many people there, but holy cow, I think we had to park a quarter mile away they were so lined up.

"So then, we sat and we timed it. About every 17 minutes, he turned out a patient.

"Not long after, I injured my back and decided to go to him. I asked him how he could possibly treat and heal people so fast.

"He just grinned and told me he used to take a little longer but he had so many people he had to hurry things up.

"Dr. André and I became friends and I started going there, now and then, just to visit.

"One time this fellow, a ball player from southern California, was carried in on a stretcher. He had been injured sliding into second base and doctors told him he would never walk again. I don't know how many times he went there, but the last time I saw him he was on crutches.

"I overheard him telling the doctor how much he loved playing baseball and hiking, and I heard Dr. André tell him, 'One more treatment and you'll be able to do both.'

"I asked Dr. André how so many people knew of him—did he advertise? 'No, I have never advertised and I don't want to!' He acted as though he was scared, even at the thought of it. He said he had enough walking advertisement all over the country and showed us letters thanking him from all over the United States."   **H. Rominger**

"I saw several people standing around two cars that had car-pooled all the way from Rochester, Minnesota. They showed me their typed up medical papers—they had been sent by the Mayo Clinic."
                                                D. Madigan

"My dad owned the Placerville Bakery. I used to see the Goat Doctor walking into town trailed by four or five milk goats.

"We would often be working after the bar next door closed at 2:00 a.m. My father always had the door open and the lights on.

"Many, many times during the night people would stop to ask directions on how to get to the Goat Doctor. They came from all over the United States.

"My father would tell them how dangerous the road was and always advised them to wait until morning.

"Our family went to him. While there, we talked with people from all over. Most of them told us other doctors had given up trying to help them.

"One man was sent there by a doctor from the San Francisco Stanford Hospital with a spinal problem.

"Frank felt up and down his spine and told him where his problem was and fixed him up fine. This was after he had been seen and x-rayed by a doctor who couldn't find his problem.

"Another guy from Medford, Oregon went in all bent over. He came out of the cabin standing straight and then began jumping up and down and hollering, 'He's a Miracle Worker!'

"I know a lot of people thought it was all a bunch of hocus-pocus. But every single case of the 10 to 12 cars before us that limped in or was even carried in came out walking and happy. And, that's the way it was."   **R. Weichold**

———————————

By 1938, several doctors from nearby towns were irate over losing patients to Frank. Most of them considered his healings lucky coincidences brought on by psychosomatic cures—more through the power of suggestion than actual treatment, or a combination of benign medication and hypnosis.

"As is usually the case, many people do not trust what they can't understand and sometimes try to discredit those who are different."   **W. Denson**

"The regular doctors didn't like the idea or understand how it (chiropractic medicine) worked, so they tried hard to get it outlawed."   **G. Fogal**

Thinking an informal hearing would be enough to close him down, the doctors arranged one. Frank received notice that a complaint had been filed against him for practicing without a license. He was to appear for a hearing before a local judge in Placerville's town hall.

On the day of the hearing, the hall filled beyond capacity with patients, doctors, and spectators. When Frank entered the building, someone let out with, "Here's the charlatan now!"

Someone else called that person a derogatory name and soon the hall was in an uproar with people hollering back and forth at one another—mostly it was the doctors arguing amongst themselves. Some called him every lowly name they could think of, while others with patients he had healed came to his defense.

"Leave him alone," yelled one doctor, "he's a good man."

When asked to take the stand, Frank walked up the aisle with a small goat in tow. After answering several questions, the Judge asked if he had anything to say.

Frank stated he considered himself a bone adjuster and that he never prescribed medication or asked payment for his services. Then he said, 'I'd like to show you something.' He laid the goat on a nearby table, put his hands on the animal's back, and with a quick movement dislocated the poor creature's spine. The goat let out a piercing, painful wail. Above the bleating, Frank challenged the doctors. "Would one of you gentlemen like to put this animal's spine back in place?"

When no one moved or said a word, he bent over the goat, quickly readjusted its spine and made the statement, "Obviously, I'm not practicing medicine as these doctors know it or they would have been able to adjust the goat's spine."

He explained to the judge his treatments differed from that of a chiropractor because he concentrated more on the pelvic region. He said he always told people with diseases to go see a medical doctor.

"There were at least 100 people there. Many that Frank had treated spoke on his behalf.

"The judge ended the hearing by saying, 'Since Mr. André only accepts donations he can not be considered a business, and therefore, can not be shut down.'

"Then he turned to Frank and said, 'If you've helped that many people, I say go to it and continue your good work, just don't call yourself a doctor, you are a healer.'" **G. Milham-Desjardin**

When the hearing was over, Frank walked back through the aisle and out the door with the little goat trailing at his heels.

Chapter Four
1940 – 1949

After the hearing, often referred to as "The Goat Trial," Frank had little more than a year of peace before he once again incurred the wrath of not only several medical doctors in and around Placerville but also a few chiropractors.

Already incensed that he had been allowed to treat people without a license, they became enraged when they saw the scores of people waiting to see him, day in and day out, and were more hell-bent than ever on shutting him down. Money was tight. Fifteen percent of the population was unemployed and taxes were at an all-time high. They felt he was taking far too many of their patients

A few doctors, trying to get "the dirt" on Frank, went to him posing as patients. They were unaware he was psychic and their covert missions were in vain.

> "He told us he used to keep a chart on each of his patients, including their addresses, until one day a group of doctors came and he caught one of them reading his patient records." **D. Cupps**

From time to time, one or two of them even went out to the cabin and more or less (politely) badgered Frank. They implied they had evidence against him for various infractions of the law.

After leaving him with threatening remarks such as, "If you don't close up shop you are going to be arrested so you had better think about it," Frank always thanked them for their concern and went about his work.

Seeing they were getting nowhere with their intimidations, the doctors again took action.

After receiving several complaints, the California State Medical Board filed a lawsuit against Frank for practicing without a license. He was served subpoenas to appear in court—which he ignored.

A warrant was issued for his arrest. But each time the official stopped at the Sheriff's office, in Placerville, to have an arresting officer accompany him, he was told the only man authorized to do this was the Sheriff and he was not available. There was always an excuse; he was out of town, his father died, or he was on vacation.

"I lived with my grandparents and my grandfather was a Sheriff for El Dorado County. The doctors were always trying to have Frank arrested. My grandfather thought the world of Frank and wasn't about to let anybody bother him." **P. Moore**

"I was a chiropractor in the Sacramento area. I had a man come by my office one cold day. He opened the door and poked his head in. He just stood there with the door open, looking around. I said to come in. He hesitated, so I said, 'Look, either come in or go out, one or the other. You're letting all the heat out!'

"So, he came in. He apologized and explained that he used to be an investigator for the AMA. He told how he had heard so much bad-mouthing about osteopaths and chiropractors, he was afraid to go to one.

"He had recently hurt his back and had seen a couple of physicians who just kept giving him pills, with one talking of back surgery. His wife had persuaded him to come to me!

"During treatment, the man happened to say, 'Have you ever heard of that fellow in the hills—the Goat Doctor?' I said yes.

"He said, 'Well, you know I went up there on three separate occasions to give him warnings and subpoenas to appear in court. The AMA was after him for practicing without a license.'

"Each time I handed him a subpoena, he just smiled and said, 'Thank you', and put the papers down on a table.

"He never did a thing. I received no cooperation at the Sheriff's office in Placerville, so I went to the DA in Sacramento.

"The head man was sitting at a desk when I first walked in and I told him I wanted an officer to go up there with me to arrest André. He stood up so abruptly I stopped in my tracks.

"Practically growling he said, 'Nobody's going to arrest the Goat Doctor!'

"I think he saw how startled I was at his outburst. He appeared to take a deep breath and gained control of himself.

"He then said, 'Sit down, I want to tell you a story'.

"He told how his very own mother had been in so much pain from a back injury and bedridden for years. Many specialists had seen her.

"After a long stay in traction at one hospital, countless pills and hundreds of dollars spent, a doctor at the Sacramento County Hospital recommended the Goat Doctor. After one treatment, she was fine.

"The DA again popped up from his chair and said, 'That man cares about people, he's a humanitarian, besides, how do you think my mother would feel if I arrested the man who made her well?'

"He pointed to the door as he growled, 'Now you get the hell out of this office and tell your people to leave that man alone! No one is going to touch him while I'm in office!'" **G. Windmiller, D.C.**

After their second unsuccessful attempt to put Frank out of business, as an annoyance some doctors began sending him their worst cases—patients they considered hopelessly incurable.

"The doctors in town would send the patients they couldn't cure to Frank. They'd say, 'Why don't you go see the Goat Doctor?' Part of the time they said it facetiously and part of the time they were dead serious." **C. Neilsen**

"While carrying one of my children, I slipped in the mud and fell. My doctor said, 'You live by the Goat Doctor don't you?' He never outright told me to go. All the doctors in the area knew of him and either respected him or were vehemently opposed to him."
L. Beckett-Pearson

"I'm not sure the exact reason, but my mother was seeing a chiropractor. Evidently, he couldn't help her because he recommended the Goat Doctor to her.

"We went there several times driving at least 40 miles each way. Although we got there in the early morning, we had to wait in a long line of cars, and then my mother would stand in a long line of people. He gave adjustments and recommended a diet that included certain herbs.

"My mother had a weak heart also. As to the results of his treatment to her, I'd have to say after seeing him she had better peace of mind."
C. Johnson

When the majority of the "incurable" patients returned healed, the doctors were astounded. Frank had gained their admiration. Now, not only did the medical community send patients they had given up on, they and their family members began going to him for their own medical care.

Eventually, even Doctor McKinnon, who filed one of the first complaints against Frank, sent patients to him and the two men became friends.

"I especially remember one time talking with a physician in the waiting area while his badly crippled wife was in with Dr. André in the treatment room.

"The physician said he had taken his wife to doctors all over Europe and no one could help her. As we visited, we took note of the time. It took 45 minutes before the woman came out of the room walking without crutches."   **V. Alexander**

"Our two-year-old daughter had some kind of problem. She was underdeveloped for her age and couldn't even sit up in a highchair to feed herself, let alone walk. We were worried sick about her.

"We had taken her to a few doctors who were of no help. We were told all sorts of things from it was a genetic disorder to she was just a lazy child. So, I took my daughter to the Goat Doctor.

"He checked her over and said it was some kind of dystrophy of the muscles and tissue. He assured us that we shouldn't worry, that in three or four months, as she grew, these would develop, and she'd be perfectly normal. He was right.

"Dr. Yanis and I were neighbors. I never mentioned taking my daughter to the Goat Doctor because I was sure he would think me crazy and I'm just as sure he never mentioned to me about sending people to the Goat Doctor because he was afraid I would think he was crazy. I would never in a million years have guessed Yanis sent people to the Goat Doctor!"   **S. Lewis, O. D.**

Originally called "Goat Doctor" by people intent on debasing Frank, he was now so-called with respect. However, in his presence more people were addressing him as Dr. André.

In hopes they might learn his methods, many doctors drove out to the cabin and asked if they might observe while he administered treatment to his patients. They were always welcome, as was anyone interested in learning from him.

Patients who witnessed the incongruous sight of one or more of these trained professionals; in their neat business attire, respectfully quiet as they observed every move made by the longhaired, barefoot, bearded mountain man in loose fitting overalls were astonished.

"I went to Mosquito several times to observe Frank at work. We became very good friends. I know he used to donate money to Father Flannigan's Home for Boys."   **G. Windmiller, D.C.**

"After sending a couple of patients to the Goat Doctor and seeing the results, I wanted to meet the man myself. I introduced myself and told him I had sent these people—even told him I considered them hopeless cases.

"He smiled and thanked me for sending them and said he was happy he could help them. He allowed me to come and observe his work.

"Frank and I became good friends. He told me when he first started treating people it was a real joy. He was happy caring for the neighbors and their children and enjoyed the cakes and sourdough bread they brought him.

"I know he used to give money to the Children's Hospital in San Francisco."   **O. Nutt, D.C.**

"As soon as I walked into the room, he looked me over and said, 'You know George you and I appear to be of the same stature.' He had me back up to him and put his hand up to feel the back of our heads. There was about a half-inch difference. He was five-feet-seven.

"I don't know how he knew, but he no more than touched me when he said, 'George, you're very interested in this work, aren't you?' I said, 'Yes I am'.

"He said, 'Anyone can do what I do and if you're as serious as I think you are, I'll teach you everything I know.' He showed me the basic practical methods he used. If a vertebra was out of place in the back, he would press firmly on the person's chest with the flat of his hand while using the thumb of his other hand to push it back in place.

"I do not remember his ever "cracking" anyone's back. Each time he would have me feel where their problem was and show me exactly what to do.

"I tried my best to store away everything he told me but I couldn't remember it all and I've regretted a thousand times over that I didn't take notes on all he said.

"What I do remember, more than anything, was the sensitiveness of those long thin fingers on his big strong hands.

"He was the most effective person to ever work on me. He was also one of the most intelligent men I ever met and could talk for hours on any subject. He was a wonderful man"   **G. Parnell,** Reflexologist

"One thing for sure, he had to have known more than they did because doctors from all over kept coming here to watch him work—trying to learn what exactly he did.

"Dr. André said he felt most of the medical practitioners were still fighting the realization of the phenomenon that the spine has more control over the whole body than people give it credit." **B. Alexander**

"I was told by my personal physician that many doctors observed his methods of treatment, but they could never discover his secret healing powers."
W. Denson

Word continued to spread about his healings and Frank was to realize just how far word-of-mouth could travel. Not only were people commuting from all over the United States, they were coming to him from Europe, South America and the Far East. It mattered little, of course, if they spoke no English.

"There were always long lines of cars. Even though the road was narrow, the people somehow managed to squeeze their vehicles in and parked on both sides.

"One time, we saw a boy who had been brought from England who could not walk. He was carried into the cabin and within minutes, he walked out."
J. Roberts

"My mother had multiple sclerosis. He recommended that once a day, she eat one cup of grated carrots and drink at least one glass of warm water. He said she should walk barefoot on the soil for one hour or longer, plus take a warm bath daily.

"The Goat Doctor helped her to the point that she was in remission for all the years until her death some 20 years later.

"One day we went there because I'd been having bad headaches. He had me sit on a stool and barely rubbed his fingers across the back of my neck. Not at all like a chiropractor had done. I have never had a headache since.

"While we were there, we met people from Germany and France, who were waiting in line to see him.

"My dad used to call him Jesus."   **D. Davidson**

"At times when I went there, I saw cars for a mile or more. I know he was recognized by people from Canada, France, and Germany."

G. Parnell, Reflexologist

"There are two incidences that are clearest in my memories.

"One was a boy from Canada who was carried in on a stretcher laying flat on his back. He walked out of the cabin within a few minutes.

"The other was an 18-year old girl I spoke with. She came from Europe. She said it was her seventh or eight time to the Goat Doctor.

"When she first came to the doctor, she was totally blind. She now had her vision back."   **I. Meadows**

"I knew a couple who would come over from their home in Hawaii. They would rent a trailer for two months and stay right out on Dr. André's property getting adjustments. They were middle-aged and came once a year for many years.

"A woman from Vancouver, Canada, would fly down, rent a car, and stay in Placerville. She would go out to Dr. André and get treatments. There would be tents pitched on the property." **G. Larson**

"A woman friend from Oakland, who worked at the Children's Hospital as a receptionist, had to sit on two pillows and was in constant pain from a tailbone injury. The doctors wanted to cut on her. She finally agreed to come up to Dr. André. I took her out to him and in one treatment she was without pain. All the tenderness was gone and she has had no problem ever again.

"While in the waiting area, a car full of Chinese people came up with a four or five-year old boy who had never been able to walk.

"Everyone in the waiting room was in tears, as well as the boy's relatives, as he wobbled out of the treatment room between his parents.

"While there, we also met a woman who came from Sweden to be treated." **M. Gersh**

"After having no success with chiropractors in Los Angeles for my bad back, I went to Dr. André. He was very kind and gentle, yet what he did was always right and I felt so much better afterwards.

"I remember the story from one fellow who went to him. He was from New York, a steel worker. He was high up on the girders when another worker fell from three stories above. He reached out and grabbed the falling man. In doing so, he injured his back. He spent all of his insurance settlement on doctors but none of them could help him.

"He came to Placerville and went to the Goat Doctor for treatment every day for a week. By the time he left here, he was well.

"Dr. André told me of a man who had come to him for treatment all the way from Iraq." **T. Hendricks**

"One time in the waiting room, we watched as a big man was helped down the hill. He was walking on his hands and feet he was so bent over. Dr. André asked if those waiting would mind and he took this man in first. Not much later, the man came out flexing his muscles and walking upright.

"He had people coming from all over the world, some from China and Iraq!" **R. Maguire**

"He had a sense of humor. When I asked him how he was able to do in one treatment what chiropractors took several treatments to do, he said, 'Many patients come from hundreds of miles away, even foreign countries. I couldn't ask them to come back three times a week.'" **C. Otis**

As he worked on people, Frank talked with them to get them to relax. They usually told of their circumstances, which again, he sensed before they spoke. Not only would he not accept money when treating the poor, often as not, he gave to them.

"He had such a gentle way about him. As he worked on people, they would tell of their circumstances. When people sounded as though they were poor and in need of help, he would not let them leave a penny and they usually went away with a box of fruit and vegetables." **L. Beckett-Pearson**

"While I was working indoors one day, a fellow from Roseville brought his daughter up. She was expecting a child and was in real pain from a sore back. She was far along in her pregnancy and could hardly walk, so I helped carry her into the treatment room and onto the table.

"On this occasion, the doctor asked me to wait, as he wanted to talk something over with me before I started working. So I went into the waiting room and began leafing through one of the many National Geographics he always had in there.

"The door was open and I couldn't help but hear every word that was said. Dr. André always engaged his patients in talk about themselves, as he went about caring for them. He said it took their minds off their problem and helped them to relax and made them easier to treat.

"In this case, the family was in a real bad financial state of affairs. The girl's husband had left her. The Doctor asked her what she did for a living.

"She said she lived with her parents. He asked her what her father did, and she said, 'Right now he's out of work because of a disability.'

"After a lengthy conversation with her, the doctor called me in. 'Orval,' he said, 'take this girl's father up to the barn and fill his gas tank!'

"Dr. André always kept gasoline in the barn for emergencies such as this, so I did. We went up to the barn and I filled the man's gas tank.

"When we got back to the house, the fellow's daughter was through with her treatment and feeling much improved.

"Dr. André had set out cases of canned beans, peas, milk, plus dried beans and fresh fruit from his trees.

"The doctor told me the reason he filled the man's tank was because he wanted to see the daughter again around the end of the week and the man had told him he didn't have the money to acquire the gas.

"The fellow offered to pay whatever he owed as soon as he got work. Dr. André said, 'You don't owe me a thing.' This sort of kindness was extended by Dr. André time-and-time again." **O. Beckett**

"During the war years, when gas was rationed, I heard him tell a fellow he should come back for another treatment. When the man said he couldn't come back because he was almost out of gas stamps, I saw the doctor give him his stamps." **A. Anderson**

"We used to go to the Goat Doctor once or twice a year. My husband had back trouble. It would get so bad he couldn't go to work.

"He'd have a treatment that would do him for a good long time but invariably, he'd put it back out. He kept my husband to where he was able to work.

"I guess he knew we weren't wealthy people and when he was through, he said there was no charge. If someone couldn't pay, that was okay with him.

"We always enjoyed going there." **C. Pederson**

"I knew this highway patrol officer, Charlie. He was chasing a car on his motorcycle and missed a sharp curve on Folsom-Auburn Road. He crashed and was in bad shape.

"He was bruised, cut up, and had broken bones all over. He couldn't walk and was in bad pain for quite some time. He was in the Sacramento Hospital and was even taken to the Mayo Clinic, but they didn't help.

"Charlie still couldn't walk and was in total misery. It was a job, but finally my friend Bill and I got Charlie into my car and hauled him over to see Frank.

"We spent the morning there. Frank put him on a table that had two or three layers of goatskins on it.

He worked on Charlie for a while, kind of gently massaging him all over for maybe 20 minutes.

"Charlie was feeling better even after the first visit. We hauled him up there a couple more times. He got Charlie in good shape and he was soon back, on regular duty with the Highway Patrol.

"Frank never charged a dime! Like most people, I couldn't believe it!"	**W. Durfey**

———————————

Prominent business and professional men, politicians, movie stars, and other celebrities were among the many wealthy people who sought Frank's help.

"I was a city policeman on the night shift most of the time. I remember that not a night went by that I was not approached by out-of-towners for directions to Dr. André's.

"There were chauffeur driven limos, Cadillacs, Lincolns, even Rolls Royces. I remember, many times, there would be foreign accents.

"Other officers on the night duty also would tell about people in fancy cars asking for directions, so it was a constant thing. They would spend the night out on the road in order to get in to see him the next day.

"If things were quiet in town, I would escort the cars to the beginning of Mosquito Road and warn the drivers that the road was a treacherous one and to be prepared for the swinging bridge."	**G. Baraque**

"I watched an obviously wealthy older woman being pushed around in a wheelchair by her chauffeur while waiting to be seen.

"When her turn came, the man pushed the wheelchair-bound woman into the cabin and came back outdoors to wait. Within a few minutes, the woman came out walking.

"The chauffeur tried to get the woman to get into the wheelchair so he could push her back up the rough grade to the car. She shooed the man away, insisting she wanted to walk.

"There were always long lines of cars parked in front of the Goat Doctor's place. The majority of the cars I saw were from San Francisco and around the Bay area."   **J. Perona**

Frank paid no attention to what people put in the donation container [at times described as a fishbowl, tin-can, box or bowl] and was often surprised at the end of the day to find just how much they had left him. These he could not hand back, but he turned down all large contributions offered to him in person.

"One day a geologist who worked for Standard Oil came in to see Dr. André.

"I thought this fellow was an alcoholic. His face was so red it looked like the blood vessels were going to burst right through the skin! His neck was swollen straight out to his chin, and he was maneuvering like he was in great pain.

"I helped get him situated on the treatment table. Dr. André asked did I mind waiting while he took care of this fellow. The doctor got him situated with hot water bottles and began manipulating the man's back.

"I could hear him, in his quiet, friendly way of talking, asking the poor fellow what exactly happened.

"The man said that he was on a job in Nevada when a big storm came up all of a sudden. The fellow that was driving was going way too fast for the muddy road. They came to a turn and the car slid right off the road!

"They hit an embankment and that threw him out over the windshield, head first, into a mud hole! He hit so hard he was knocked unconscious. The fellows that were with him didn't even bother to pull him out at first.

"They thought he was dead! His story was that he was there for several minutes before he began to come to and then struggled around a bit before they got him out of the hole.

"He named all sorts of doctors and medical establishments he'd been to since the accident, which had actually happened months before. But his condition was virtually the same as the day he was injured.

"He came to Dr. André on a Saturday and after his treatment, the doctor said he'd like to see him again the following Monday.

"I was there when he returned. I did not recognize him, the inflammation had left his face and the swelling was almost totally gone. He could turn his head clear around to the side! Dr. André asked him how he felt.

"'It's a little sore,' he replied, 'but it's the first time I've been able to bend my neck since the accident!'

"After the doctor gave him another treatment and said he was finished, the man asked how much he owed.

"The doctor gave his usual reply, 'you can leave a donation in the amount you feel it to be worth in the plate by the door.'

"Well, that fellow was dumbfounded by this remark. He turned to his wife and asked that she give him his checkbook that she carried in her purse.

"Then he proceeded to write out a check with five digits in it that Dr. André didn't want to accept. I think it was for two hundred dollars.

"He told Dr. André, 'This is the first time in months that I've been without pain and felt this good! The company I work for has put out thousands of dollars to hospitals and doctors trying to get me well, not to mention the thousands I've paid out myself. None gave me relief from pain. Now, after just two visits to you, I am free of pain and totally comfortable! So this still doesn't pay for what it's worth to me!'

"Frank tried to refuse the check, but the man was so adamant in wanting to pay that he finally took it, but I doubt that he cashed it.

"Within a couple of weeks, the man returned. This time he came with an offer to build a hospital or clinic for Frank in town.

"But, Frank did not want to leave here. He said he was afraid if he left Andréville, he would lose his touch.

"It was only a couple of weeks later that another doctor came, and after observing Frank's work and success, offered to build Frank a clinic and was turned down.

"He returned for another visit. After the session, the two men walked to the outer door of the cabin and stopped in the doorway.

"On seeing the scores of people patiently waiting to be seen, the visitor decided to broach the subject again. 'Just think how many more people you could administer to if you had your own hospital in a city,' he said. Frank smiled and said, 'No, thank you just the same.'

"After a long pause and not wanting to give up, the visitor pushed a little further. 'Just think how much easier it would be for people to find you.'

"Frank didn't say a word during the few moments it took for his eyes to take in the view of the road with all the people waiting in and around their cars, sitting on benches indoors and out, and grouped around his garden.

"Then with a broad grin he said, 'I think enough of them have found me already!'"   **O. Beckett**

"I used to sit and visit an old neighbor in Citrus Heights. He told me how his granddaughter, who lived with her wealthy parents in Nebraska, had become a cripple after sliding down the banister and crashing into the newel post at the bottom of the stairs, hurting her pelvis. It had even stunted her growth. The father heard of the Goat Doctor, so he took a week's vacation, specifically to bring his daughter to see him.

"When the father began telling him how she had become crippled, the Goat Doctor said, 'I know all about it.'

"He cared for the girl for approximately one and one-half hours. She came out walking. The man gave the Goat Doctor a signed, blank check and told him he was quite wealthy and to write in any amount.

"The doctor wrote in the same small amount he suggested to any patient at that time.

"The man wrote a letter of appreciation to Dr. André. He basically held the doctor in awe, as they had spent a fortune on so many medical doctors and specialists without a trace of improvement."   **T. Mustra**

"It was two or three weeks after the doctor treated and healed him that this wealthy man showed up at the cabin driving a brand-new Cadillac he had brought to give to the doctor. The man's chauffeur had followed the Cadillac in his employer's car all the way from San Francisco to drive him back home, but the doctor wouldn't accept it.

"Another time I was there a police officer came in to be healed. He wrote out a check for one thousand dollars because he was so thankful for being made well." **T. Lester**

"I don't remember the reason for my father-in-law's visit to the Goat Doctor, but what I do remember is the story he told me.

"He had seen a man hobbling into the cabin with the aid of crutches and within minutes, the man came out the cabin door. He was all smiles and carrying his crutches.

"The man stopped to talk with my father-in-law and a few other people who were lingering about. He told how he and his wife had driven several hundred miles after being told of the Goat Doctor by an osteopath, who had given up on treating him.

"The man said he was absolutely stupefied at such sudden and positive results. Not only that, the man was so thankful he told the Goat Doctor he would like to buy him a brand-new automobile—any car he cared to choose.

"The Goat Doctor told him, 'No thank you. That won't be necessary, but if you would like to leave a donation, you can put something in the bowl on the table near the door.'

"The man said he tried to tell the doctor he was serious about the car, but the doctor just smiled and told the man he appreciated the offer." **D. Thompsen**

"My father used to take treatment from Frank. We got well acquainted with the Andrés.

"This wealthy man had taken his daughter to all kinds of doctors and specialists because she had no feelings in her legs. He brought her to André a few times. Then André told him, 'You won't have to come back again. You might have some trouble with your daughter on the way home. She may be in a great deal of pain but I've done all I can do for her.'

"On the way home, she began to yell and scream. A short time later, she walked.

"The man went back to see Frank and wanted to give him anything he wanted, but Frank just told him seeing her happy was payment enough."   **L. Croft**

More vehicles than ever parked along Mosquito Road in front of the Andrés' place. Along with the cars, trucks, and travel trailers, waiting their turn in line were ambulances from San Francisco, Sacramento, Placerville, Auburn, Grass Valley, and Folsom hospitals. They brought patients who had been bedridden for weeks and months. Those with emergency cases had to weave their way in and out of the parked cars and they were always seen first.

"While there, not only did I see cars and trucks lined up forever, there were at least three or four ambulances from various cities. They were waiting in line with bedridden patients.

"I watched as they wheeled those patients down the hill on gurneys and into the Goat Doctor's cabin. A short while later, those same people came walking out under their own steam. It was unbelievable!"
W. Langton

"After my son was born in Sacramento, my pelvic area didn't mesh back together correctly. I couldn't walk, not even to go potty.

"First off, the doctor in Sacramento put me in a corset, and after that I was taped, then I was seen by a specialist from San Francisco. Both doctors said I'd never walk again.

"At the end of six months, I was still in tape and unable to walk. The last doctor I saw wanted to put me in a cast.

"My aunt, uncle, and grandfather had at one time or another been treated by the Goat Doctor and suggested I go to him. My mother and father had me taken there by ambulance.

"The doctor checked me over and said, 'Don't worry, you'll be fine.' He treated me for about a half hour on three different occasions. The third time, I was able to stand and walk. I was cured!

"He told me if the doctors had put me in a cast, the nerve ends would have deteriorated to the point that I would have been paralyzed. I feel I owe my life to him."   **E. Buth**

"Because my grandfather and Frank were such good friend I went there over a dozen times.

"I am not exaggerating when I tell you one day I saw at least six ambulances parked along the road. They were from all different cities."   **P. Moore**

"I saw people being brought to Frank in ambulances. They were carried down the hill and into his cabin on stretchers.

"I saw these people come out unaided and walk back up the hill to get into the waiting ambulances."
J. D. Lawson

Frank did not like to work on people who had had surgery or bones that had healed out of place. He was afraid it could make matters worse but sometimes he made an exception.

"For five years, I wore a back brace and was in chronic pain. I had been in a car accident while in the service. My husband, a friend, and myself, decided to go to the Goat Doctor to see what he could do for my back and my friend's arthritis.

"As we walked down the path from the road, we could see the Goat Doctor's mother sitting out in front of the waiting room on a crude bench made from two wooden boxes with a plank of wood for the seat.

"We were clued in that we would be taken in order of arrival, being warned by someone in the line that the Goat Doctor was known to come out and say, 'I'm not seeing anyone else today', if he heard any squabbling as to who was next.

"When my turn came, the Goat Doctor had me get up on his treatment table, which was covered with goat hides. It was an unbelievable scenario. The man had dark piercing eyes, salt and pepper gray hair pulled back in a ponytail by a rubber band. He had on old bib overalls and yet, he had a Christ-like appearance.

"He sensed without my telling him that I had had surgery on my back. He hesitated at first, saying he did not like to work on anyone who had had surgery.

"But after he felt up and down my spine a couple of times, he decided it would be okay. He did some gentle manipulating on my back then had me step down from the table.

"'Now bend down and touch your toes.' he said. I didn't think I could as I had not been able to for years. 'Just try,' he said, and I did. It hurt some, but I could do it. He had worked wonders. In just those few minutes, he changed my life.

"I walked out carrying that big old brace under my arm, with the undergarment straps hanging down, with all the waiting people watching. I didn't care. It felt so good to be able to walk without it on my back.

"Upon reaching the outer door, I placed money in a tin can nailed to the wall for donations.

"After my treatment, the Goat Doctor told his helper he was going to take a short break. I asked if it were a coffee break and he said no, he would be eating an orange and drinking a glass of goat's milk.

"My friend went in for her turn next. She was in and out within a few minutes. Her first words to us were, 'I'm going to have a lot of happy friends!'

"She said she had told the Goat Doctor of her pain from arthritis.

"'That's easy' he said, 'cut out eating processed sugar.'

"'But I just canned umpteen jars of fruit with sugar.'

"'Give them away to your friends!' he said.

"An elderly black man caught our attention earlier mainly because of the eyeglasses he wore. They appeared as thick as the bottom of Coke bottles. We had walked ahead and talked with him for a few minutes while waiting our turn. He said his children were the brightest things in his life but they were now grown and he was all alone.

"He told us how much he enjoyed reading, however his eyesight was all but gone. In leaving, we were about to pass him when we saw him sitting on an outside bench with his glasses in his hand.

"He said, 'I see he fixed you up all right.'

"I said, 'Yes, it's unbelievable. How did you fare?'

"He said he just couldn't believe it. After a short visit with this man, who had done some fiddling with his neck, he could now see clearly without the aid of glasses. He held his glasses up and snapped them in half.

"After we had gotten a little ways away from the Goat Doctor's place, I hollered out, 'Stop the car!' to my husband.

"He slammed on the brakes and said, 'What in the world is the matter?'

"We had come to the road entering a deserted lumber mill. I said, 'I have to get out.'

"'Are you hurting?' he asks.

"'No, I just want to run around the car a few times. I want to test my back just in case it goes out, so I can go right back and have him fix it again.'"   **F. Matzka**

"I had injured my pelvic bone in a fall and was in chronic pain. My doctor had let it heal out of place, saying it wasn't broken. I went to the Goat Doctor.

"He felt the area and immediately told me what was wrong. He said he would have to hurt me if he were to help me and that he would have to re-break the pelvic bone and set it correctly.

"I gave my approval. The Goat Doctor then left me and went into another room to meditate. When he returned, he was holding his hands up like a surgeon. He said this was to keep his energy strong.

"'Now, this is going to hurt,' he again said.

"His strong hands took hold and with a quick and careful snap, he separated the pelvic where it had previously been broken. At the sound of the snap of the bone, I let out a howl.

"I remember his teasing, 'Now look what you did. You've scared all my goats away!' I spent three weeks in bed to heal, and have been fine since."   **N. Smith**

"As a little girl, I had gone to Dr. André to feed the goats while my uncle got a treatment. At 19 years of age, I was in a car accident. My back was paralyzed and I had no control over my bladder. I had broken ribs and burns on my upper back.

"I spent two months in the Placerville Sanitarium, then was sent to a San Francisco hospital. I was put into weights and traction with little other care. Their prognosis: I would never sit up or have children.

"Two months after leaving the hospital, my uncle and his wife came by and put me into their car. I was in such pain that I could not bend to sit. My aunt sat in the back seat to hold me in a lying position for the very difficult trip out Mosquito Road.

"The doctor didn't like people driving on the dirt road in front of the cabin, but he let us because it was such a long way down the hill to pack me.

"On my first visit there, he doctor told me he was sorry but he didn't think he could treat me. He said things had healed out of place for too long a time.

"His mother came into the room and walked all around the treatment table I was laying on. She didn't touch me; she just looked me over real good.

"Then she told her son, 'I feel you can help her, go ahead.' So he said he would try.

"He was so gentle in manipulating me and so nice. He told me he could only make me feel better for a short period of time. I always felt so good after going there and after the second treatment I was able to sit up in the car for the drive home. I had not sat upright for eight months.

"Dr. André told me if I had been able to get to him earlier, I would have been able to walk, but the weights had pulled my muscles out of alignment and over six months had gone by. My bladder and kidney system were restored early on during his treatments.

"Sometimes we couldn't get there 'til eight thirty or nine at night. My husband would help care for the goats by putting them in the barn for the night.

"Frank would carry a baby goat down for me to hold when I would sit with Mother André and wait for them to tend the goats. Except for when the roads were closed in the wintertime, I went to him once a week every week for six years.

"Although most people were giving him around two dollars and fifty cents at the time, he never had us pay him a cent. So my husband and I would pick up the André's mail, buy and deliver their groceries, and do errands for them.

"Five years after first seeing him, I had my first child. Dr. André wanted me to have it naturally so that the sense of feeling would come back into my limbs. But the medical doctors had their way, so I wasn't made to use my own muscles as much as I should have to deliver.

"I remember one girl who went to him had been in a car accident and was told by several doctors she would never walk again. After a few visits to Dr. André, she did in fact walk across the stage to receive her high school diploma. Everyone applauded extra for her in doing so." **P. DeWolfe**

"One time, after driving over an hour and a half to get there, and waiting 12 hours for our turn, he asked if we minded waiting for a while longer.

"Someone had brought in a boy of about ten years of age. He had gotten hurt so badly he couldn't walk or stand. Frank said he had to break the boy's bones and reset them straight." **D. Cupps**

By 1945, helicopters were bringing patients to a site not far from the cabin where ambulances and other vehicles sat in wait for patients.

"On our way to the doctors we saw a helicopter land in an area we were told was a deserted lumber mill. Someone said it landed there occasionally and that it belonged to a hospital. It carried a crippled girl and an emergency vehicle was there at the site waiting to transport her the Goat Doctor's place.

"The Goat Doctor had her carried right in. We were there to see her walk out of the cabin."

F. Matzka

"I was there one day when a helicopter landed a ways down the road.

"A boy was in critical condition from some kind of accident. He was carried into the cabin on a stretcher. After a half hour with the Goat Doctor, he came out walking. Everybody began cheering and screaming.

"Dr. André looked like Jesus—to me he was God!"

M. Zalutka

The increased workload became too much for Frank. On a large piece of galvanized metal, he had a sign painted indicating working hours. It was nailed onto two closely spaced pine trees they called the "Twin Pines" in front and off to the right of the cabin. The black letters and numbers on a background of white were large enough to be read from the road. The sign indicated the waiting room door would open at 8 a.m. and close at 4 p.m., Monday through Saturday. Frank stopped taking patients at four o'clock so he could be finished around five.

"My Mother took me to him when I was a child. I had problems because one leg was two or three inches shorter then the other. He corrected the problem.

"I remember him wearing a red bandana, such as railroad workers wore. It was rolled and tied around his forehead like a sweatband.

"I recall seeing him walking up to the road from the cabin, one or two hours before he was due to stop working, so he could check the cars for the most serious cases and care for them before day's end.

"I also recall seeing the one and only picture in the cabin. It was of a wolf on a hill looking down on sheep."   **D. Radcliff**

"I remember he used to go up the hill and check out the people along the road, to see who was worse off, so he could take them in before he closed for the day. This was before he got too busy." **B. Olenslager**

"We waited our turn in line for several hours and thought we would be seen that day. We knew the doctor stopped taking patients at 4 p.m.

"At three o'clock, the doctor's helper came out and told everyone that was all he would be seeing that day. We didn't know that he did not believe in setting clocks for daylight savings time. To him it was four o'clock. We had to stay overnight. When we awoke, there were 13 cars more cars in line.

"My back was bad. Dr. André had me bend over to do an adjustment to my spine. Within a couple of minutes of painless manipulation, there was a big snap from my back and I was fine. As I walked out of his treatment room and past the waiting room full of patients, I heard someone say, 'There goes another one!'

"Off to one side of the cabin, I couldn't help but notice a large pile of crutches and braces that people had discarded." **A. Kattenhorn**

"Frank was a very happy person. He loved people and was very happy with his Mother and Father.

"Sundays and after work, he spent time in his garden, tended his goats and sometimes took photos, which he developed himself. I don't remember ever hearing of him fishing or gold mining for recreation in the river nearby as so many of the folks here did.

"During the Second World War, I never heard him say a word about what was going on. Frank's attitude was total peace, with himself and the rest of the world and it all came through." **V. Alexander**

"We had a mutual friend of the doctor's so we got to see him on a Sunday. I had one leg shorter than the other but the Goat Doctor fixed me up fine." **L. Loudon**

Driving the rough and dangerous Mosquito Road was difficult for anyone. It was especially trying for people in pain making their way to the Goat Doctor but it did not stop them from coming.

"One time I was in a motorcycle wreck, injuring my back in the right kidney area. I went to the Goat Doctor for an adjustment on a Sunday. The result was fabulous. I paid him two dollars.

"Another time I went there for treatment for my hip. It was eight miles northeast of Placerville down grade to the American River and steep up the other side with many hairpin curves on a rough road.

"I was riding my 1939, 14 cubic-inch Indian motorcycle. On my way home, I hit a bump and could feel my hip jerk out of place again." *C. Otis*

"You could go out there with a bad back and have a treatment that fixed you up, but the drive home on that rough road would put your back out again."

R. Weichold

"We remember driving that horrible road one day. A big lumber truck came barreling down the hill, almost hitting us. We got the crap scared out of us."

A. Kattenhorn

"My husband went to him many times, but probably only had him "adjust" his back two times. He really helped him. I used to enjoy talking to both him and his mother. The inside of his house had goatskins on the furniture, the floors, and the walls.

"The road out there was not all that good in those days. Friends of ours who were going to him for treatments, went over the bank into the river and were killed." **C. Scheiber**

"We were scared to death of that horrible road and I used to get carsick. When we had to go with our parents to the Goat Doctor's, my sister, and brother and I used to lie on the floor of the car." **I. Worth**

"One time, my father was suffering from severe back pain. He wasn't a drinking man, but because he was in such pain and we'd told him about the rough road, he drank some whiskey to numb the pain.

"After treating him, Dr. André said to him, ' If you ever come back, DON'T have liquor on your breath.'"

G. Parnell, Reflexologist

"I had to do the driving, and during those days the road to the Goat Doctor's house was so terrible that both of us felt that if you didn't before that day, you'd surely have a back problem by the time you arrived."

L. Oakes

"My mother had a bad back. My uncle and my dad packed my mother, sister, and me into the car very early in the morning.

"We were off to find the Goat Doctor, a man shrouded in mystery! We took a large basket of food, as it was to be a full day's outing. My father checked the tires and the brakes on the car as he had heard it was a rough road.

"He didn't want to tell us how most of the way from Placerville to Mosquito was all hairpin curves. Although I don't think he knew quite how rugged the whole trip would be, because as well planned and careful as my father was, the car slid off the side of the muddy dirt road.

"After getting back on the road, my uncle and my father bantered back and forth, as to whether or not they should go any farther. But they'd talked about the trip so long that I sensed they would.

"My father had taken my mother to several conventional medical men to no avail. He just happened to hear from someone about the Goat Doctor. It was a desperate and last resort attempt in seeking help for my mother.

"It was an all day trip—very scary and dangerous. We did not get home until late at night. My mother's back was fine after his treatments and stayed fine till very old."

J. Piiru

"The road out to his place was precarious. It was a bad road, to say the least. My friend was in so much

pain that he yelled every time we hit a bump, and
that was all the time."   **A. Williams**

"There was always a car stopped along the road
with either a flat tire, stuck in the mud or where
someone had missed a curve and smashed into a
tree."   **T. Anderson**

In desperation, a group of local residents formed a protest
committee with Orval as spokesman to persuade the county
to pave the road from the bridge to the André's place.

While attending a County Supervisors meeting, they
were told a petition with 200 signatures was needed. On
hearing this, one man laughed and said, "That's easy, just
take the petition over to the Goat Doctors."

The signatures were obtained within two days in the
Goat Doctor's waiting room!

Because Mosquito was so hard to get to, from Placerville,
the Sheriff made Orval an on-call honorary deputy, for the
area.

One story yet circulating around Placerville is that
Frank would go into the Sheriff's office once a year and
plunk down a bundle of money, as much as $5,000, on a
counter or desk. Supposedly, this was to placate the
department for having to take care of the traffic in front of
his place.

"I don't believe for a minute the story about Frank
paying money to the Sheriff's office. If he did, it had
to be that pressures forced him to. We all have our
limits."   **C. Neilsen**

"We never heard of any trouble at his place. The only time the game warden came around was when he needed an adjustment on his back!" **B. Alexander**

———————————

At times, there were patients with more severe medical problems who needed ongoing treatment for periods of days or even weeks. Frank, now too busy to do it himself, bought lumber and hired carpenters to build some cabins behind and to the left of the barn.

Most people referred to the crudely built, unpainted and rustic looking cabins as sheds or shacks.

"Frank had cabins built on the land. These were to house people who had medical problems that would take several treatments to correct, and, at times were used for a helper or a caretaker.

"As clean as the place was to me, it always smelled like Angora Goats." **J. D. Lawson**

"There were three or four small buildings on the place. Except for one that had two rooms, they were just one-room shacks. The Andrés liked to refer to the larger one as the 'guest cottage'."

L. Beckett-Pearson

———————————

Through the years Anna's health continued to fail and Frank took over the cooking and cleaning for the family. Patients and friends helped some, but hired help eventually became necessary.

"I did house work for the Andrés for several months. I worked once a week for four to five hours.

"I had to gather up all the goatskins that were used as rugs, take them out to the back porch, lean over the railings and give them a good shaking. The rugs were so heavy I was always afraid I would go over the railing. This was scary because below the porch was at least a twenty-foot drop off a steep embankment that ended in Mosquito Creek.

"After I shook the goatskins, I cleaned the linoleum floors with a mixture of water and sheep dip. When the floors were dry, I'd bring the goatskins back in and put them all over the floor.

"I remember how hot the kitchen always was. The kitchen wood stove was kept burning all year round to heat water for the hot water bottles Frank used on patients.

"Except for a slight odor of the sheep dip, the house had a good smell. Something was always cooking on the stove, usually stew or soup made of goat or chicken meat."   **L. Beckett-Pearson**

"I remember his mother walking around the room with a feather duster, dusting everything in sight. Anna constantly had things for Frank to do. Besides his patients, he cared for the chickens and goats.

A. Boeding

One day, a woman was brought to Frank in a wheelchair. Her name was Bertha Packard. She was short and stocky and wore her hair braided on top of her head. She had a bad hip from an automobile accident.

As he worked on Anna, she told Frank she had no money to pay him. He told her not to be concerned about that.

Frank must have liked Bertha, because after healing her, he hired her as a cook and housekeeper.

She turned out to be a very good cook and the Andrés had company for Sunday visits and meals more often than before. Bertha lived in the guest cottage and worked for the Andrés for several years.

"We used to enjoy going over to Mosquito to visit my grandmother Bertha.

"She always had so many interesting tales about the people that went there.

"She stayed with the family until about a year or so before she died."		**J. Moss**

Bertha Packard

Bertha (standing), Ernest, Frank, and friends

There was always work to be-done—indoors and out. Even the linoleum in the treatment room had to be replaced two or three times a year, because of so much foot-traffic.

Most caretakers hired to help with the goats, outside chores and carpentry work, were patients down on their luck. A Mr. Gould was hired, but worked only a couple of weeks before dying on the property.

Frank then hired a carpenter to do some renovating.

Taking space from the kitchen, a room was built behind Anna's bedroom for patients to rest after treatments. You could barely walk into the room it was so small; a single bed took up most of the space.

> "It was really something to see. Frank would be working on a patient in the treatment room, while another patient lay on a cot nearby, relaxing their muscles with hot water bottles. In another room, a third person lay on a bed resting after their treatment.
> "Some were real bad off, and yet the bulk of them were fixed in one treatment." **C. Bovey**

At the other end of the kitchen, a bathroom was built for the family. It was of adequate size with a sink, toilet, and crowfoot tub. Patients still used the outhouse.

> "Sensing the call of nature, Dr. André's helper directed me to the outhouse. My husband used to laugh at how scared I got when I had to use the two-seater behind the cabin. It was scary in the fact that at least half of the building jutted out into space. Through the two holes was pure daylight, with earth quite a ways below.
> "I was afraid the outhouse would topple over if I went in. My husband tried to assure me that he could

see it was safely built with the majority of the building's weight secured to earth." **F. Matzka**

"The outhouse jutted out over an embankment. Through the holes, you saw air. The chickens and other fowl would clean up the mess below." **E. Teany**

Frank managed to spend some time each day with the goats. After closing the "repair shop", as he liked to refer to the treatment room, he would milk a few goats. He said it helped him to relax.

Frank and friend inside the barn (courtesy of David A.)

"Every now and then, I'd see Dr. André up on the side of the hill with the goats. He'd have his arm around a goat's neck or patting one on it's back while talking to it.

"He'd be frolicking about like a kid, 'scuse the pun', playfully roughhousing with them. He sure stunk like a goat afterwards." **J. Perona**

"Everyday, wearing knee-high rubber boots, Frank would take out his flock of goats to feed on the mountain's grassy slopes.

"He was as agile as a mountain goat jumping off a 15-foot cliff by his home. After he returned home, he'd lock up the goats and then take care of his customers." **T. Budnik**

"When he had TB, he said one of the reasons he got the goats was to keep his mind off of being sick. 'You know, one goes this way, the other that, and it keeps me busy keeping them together.' He told me at night he had to gather them up from the canyons and put them in the barn because the coyotes were so bad. By that time, he said, 'I was so tired I went to bed and slept all night.'" **H. Rominger**

———————

A large area around the goat barn was fenced and some of the goats remained there during the day. When the gate to the corral was left open someone usually regretted it.

If a car door was open as little as three or four inches, the goats were known to get in and do real damage. The neighbors seldom complained because the goats ate a lot of the dry brush and weeds that were such fire hazards.

"We lived in a house near the Goat Doctor's place. My father-in-law was living with us. One day when I got home from work, my father-in-law came up to me and said, 'One of the goats came up here, and you know that da-da-damn-damned goat was in the house.' (He stuttered a little bit.)

"We had a folding ladder coming down from the attic and the goat even got up there. He said, 'I chased that thing up and down, all over the place. I guess it finally got the idea and left.'

"My father-in-law asked, 'Is there any way you can talk to Mrs. André down there to keep them goats off?'

"I said, 'I'll talk to her when I see her.' I told her about it and she got the biggest kick out of it, really. Of course, I told her I wasn't mad about it at all."

M. Pearson

"Frank told us about giving a man money to have upholstery work done, after one of his pet goats made lunch out of the back seat of the man's car."

G. Milham-Desjardin

"I came home from school one day and could hear my mother yelling and screaming to beat the band.

"She'd left a door open and was out doing chores. Several goats had gotten inside the house.

"They were upstairs and down and had eaten up all the plants and various items. She was chasing them with a broom." **C. Marshall**

"I was surveying on the Goat Doctor's property. One of the goats jumped on the hood of my truck and put dents in it." **R. Reese**

"No matter what, come hell or high water, the Goat Doctor was always kind and patient, but if any of the children started messing around with his goats, he closed up shop right then."   **M. Zalutka**

Frank had as many as 90 goats at a time. He had Angora, Alpine, and Pigmy goats, but most of his herd was Nubian, as they were hardy and preferred in areas like Mosquito where forage and roughage was plentiful.

He usually kept between one to two dozen Angoras, because he considered their milk to be the most healthful, and the oil from their fur to have stronger healing qualities.

Most of the billy goats were not around very long as they were raised for the sale of meat. Only a few males, kept for breeding stock, had a longer life span. The nanny goats, used for their milk and reproduction, were kept for years. They were given names and allowed to roam around the cabin, along with the André's one or two dogs, several cats, chickens, guinea hens, and peacocks.

Every so often, someone showed up at the cabin with an injured pet, thinking "Goat Doctor" meant veterinarian.

"The first time I heard of the Goat Doctor was when my sister who lived in the Placerville area, stopped by for a visit. I was in pain after injuring my back. She suggested I come up and see this Goat Doctor. She said that all her husband's fellow workers at PG&E went to him.

"She told me one of the men first heard of him from people who had taken their dogs to him."
H. Rominger

"I was about ten or eleven years old when my dog, a cocker spaniel, got hurt. I don't know why, but he couldn't jump. My mother took the dog to Dr. André. He ran his hands down the spine, touching here and there.   The dog was better immediately—no more problems."   **Lucky Nelson**

"We had a very close friend in Placerville who had a little Doxie. He and his wife and dog were in an auto accident.

"From that day on the Doxie couldn't stand on her hind feet. They took her to the vet, but he didn't do any good.

"Someone   suggested   they   take   her   to   a chiropractor, but they were afraid people would laugh at them. They decided it wouldn't hurt to ask Frank. He said to bring the dog in after he was closed.

"The doctor twisted the dog a couple of times and the dog jumped down and ran all around."

L. Beckett-Pearson

Frank was often seen walking on his property carrying a bucket. People thought nothing more of it than maybe he was taking feed to a sick goat.

Until, one day, a neighbor saw him crossing the road and noticed how taut the muscles were on his arm, which made the bucket appear to be extra heavy.

The neighbor obviously startled Frank when he called out "hello" to him, because he said Frank's head spun around real fast and the look on his face could only be described as the proverbial saying goes, 'a little boy caught with his hand in a cookie jar'.

Many patients told of seeing a bucket or two of coins under Frank's treatment table, so when word got out that he had been seen burying something in the ground from a bucket, it did not take much to put two-and-two together.

From that day on, people appeared to look at the ground more than usual when on his property.

"We lived in Davis at the time. My Dad used to go to the Goat Doctor who had an Indian woman with braided hair working about the place.

"I remember walking around the property waiting for my father. We siblings would walk down to a sort of wash that was by the side of the Goat Doctor's house.

"We had heard tales of the Goat Doctor burying his money, so we walked along kicking rocks, looking for money, and watching out for snakes. We kept looking at a certain tree, thinking, 'That's where he buried it—under that pine tree!'"   **D. Montgomery**

———————

By this time, the Andrés no longer sold fruit and vegetables but continued selling goat products for their livelihood. The only money used from donations, was that needed to improve conditions or in some way aided in the caring of patients.

Most donations given to Frank were in the form of coins. Some of the currency received he deposited in the bank and some he had exchanged for rolls of silver.

"Orval often took Frank's deposits to the bank. The bank, in turn, would mail the receipts back to the doctor. One day, Orval was on his way to Placerville, and as was his habit, he stopped at the Goat Doctor's place to see if there was anything he needed from town.

"As he entered the house, he saw Dr. André putting the lid on a quart jar (a regular canning jar) that was full of money. The doctor called him over to the fireplace, saying, 'I want you to see this—I have to trust someone.'

"Dr. André then proceeded to remove a stone from the hearth, exposing a cavity in the dirt beneath. In that cavity, Orval saw a big earthen jar, and he could also see two other fruit jars full of money.

"The doctor told him that if anything ever happened to him he wanted Orval to see that his adoptive parents received the money. He said that no one else knew about it. Orval promised he would carry out his wishes." **L. Beckett-Pearson**
L. Davies - Mosquito Memories

"I worked at Bank of America in Placerville and Frank André used to come in carrying a large sack full of money.

"I had to take him into a back room because it took such a long time to count his deposit. There were thousands of dollars in the sack." **L. Schroth**

"Occasionally, Frank would ask my wife to take money to his bank on her weekly trip to town. If Ernest knew about it, he would usually get her aside and ask her to pick up some hard-rock candy for Anna and a bottle of good booze for himself.

"My wife knew Anna and Frank didn't like him drinking it, but Ernest would soft-soap her by telling her it was for some medical reason. He wasn't a big drinker — he just liked a nip now and again." **J. D. Lawson**

Although Frank had been treating patients for over 20 years, there were times when he was not sure of himself and would ask Anna's opinion. Just as often, Anna offered her advice without his asking. There were times she told him what was wrong with a person as they walked down the path from the road, even before they got near the cabin.

"I'd seen her call out to Frank from her room to where he was treating someone. I don't think she could even hear and she'd tell him this or that was the person's ailment. She didn't talk to them or touch them."   **O. Beckett**

"One time there, we heard Frank tell a patient, 'I can't help you.' He did not want to touch the man who was lying on the treatment table. Hearing what he had said, his mother walked over and around the table, looking at the man from different angles.

"She walked into another room for a few minutes to pray. She came back out and told Frank, 'Yes you can help him.'"   **C. Bovey**

"Many times when Dr. André just didn't seem to be able to get the results he wanted, he would go in and talk to his mother or she would even appear in the room and make a comment or two on where he should work, and immediately he would get results."   **R. Maguire**

"A couple of times when I was there, Frank went to the door of his mother's room and asked her to please come out and look at a patient. He would consult with her when he wasn't quite sure of his findings."   **D. Cupps**

"I was quite impressed by the mother. I felt she had a tremendous influence on reassuring him of his ability to help someone."   **D. Dodge**

"We lived in Portola at the time. One day while ice-skating, my sister fell, landing on her tailbone. She was 13 years of age. She was in such pain and wasn't able to walk without my mother's help. She had been to regular doctors for treatment, but they said they couldn't help her.

"My parents were in the midst of buying property in Pleasant Valley near Mosquito. Everyone around there knew of the Goat Doctor.

"After listening to the different stories about him, my aunt got the directions and we took my sister there to see him. It was still nighttime and dark when we got in line behind other cars in front of the Goat Doctor's place. We were seen around two in the afternoon the next day.

"Dr. André checked my sister over and told my mother he was very sorry he could not help her. He said the bone had been broken and left to heal out of line for too long of time.

"With all hope of my sister being made well now gone, my mother, sister and I were preparing to leave when the doctor's mother asked us to come with her.

"She took us into another room and told my mother, 'I think we can help your girl. Now what I want you to do is this. Take a large bath towel, soak it in hot water, and put it on your girl's back for at least one hour a day for two weeks. Bring her back to us within a day of doing this.' My mother did exactly as Mrs. André said.

"When we returned, Dr. André helped my sister onto the treatment table. He did some kind of massage or manipulation on her that put her pelvic bone back into alignment.

"It took a little while but by the time he finished, she was fine. She never ever had another problem with it.

"The Goat Doctor was a contributing factor when my parents later decided to move to the Placerville area."   **C. Bashline**

"His mother was a driving force. She used to sit in a rocker in her room and watch the people come down the path. From this she would tell the Goat Doctor what a person's ailment was." **D. Silva**

"Mrs. André was almost always on a cot in the corner of the room and she would diagnose what should be done.

"Now, she did not have to have the patient in the room. Somebody would ask her about someone that was not there at the time and she could tell what the person needed.

"She was like Edgar Cayce, but she only prescribed herb teas and things like that." **E. Clark**

"My stepfather went to the Goat Doctor. He was very impressed with Dr. André's mother who was at times on hand when a patient was so bad they would see Mother André first before the treatment. If she felt her son could not help she would tell them so, and he never worked on them in that case.

"Very few times, I understand, did this happen, for he was able to help very severe cases.

"Frank acknowledged to us that his mother was able to determine if a serious case could be helped or not just by looking at the person." **G. Bottenberg**

"We felt their healings were to do mainly with being psychic. Many times Frank would have someone on the table in the treatment room and Mother André would call out to him from her room telling him he needed to do this or that.

"Sometimes she told him an exercise the person should do or a certain kind of herb they should use or that they should go barefoot in the dirt or sleep on pine needles. The thing was she was nowhere near the people. She would barely see them walk by her door!

"One day, Father André said to me, 'You know my dear, the most critical part of the treatment is to have the patients come in here and wait while sitting on these goatskins, totally ignoring each other and then have a hen lay an egg in their lap.'" **C. Neilsen**

Anna, now in her seventies, never recovered from the injury to her back. Some days she could barely hobble around. On her bad days, Frank would carry her into the treatment room and lay her on the resting cot. This allowed Anna to visit with people and Frank could keep an eye on her.

It did not matter how many patients he had Anna always came first! Frank not only loved Anna, he cherished her. No mother could have had a more adoring son.

Anna

"Frank called her 'Mumsy'. He took such good care of her. After her health worsened, he cleaned and cooked for her. He was all that kept her alive in her later years. If she had a headache, he'd give her a treatment right away. He was absolutely devoted to her." **L. Croft**

"Anna was usually propped up on pillows in her bed or on the cot in the treatment room. She was very fragile. When she was in the treatment room, she could be quite talkative." **C. Neilsen**

"I never saw his mother standing. She was always lying down. The word was she was born with a veil. She would tell Frank if he could or could not help someone." **J. Dixon**

"Francis André lived with this real old couple. The woman was down flat on her back and couldn't get out of bed. He treated her and the first thing you know she was up-and-about again." **C. Otis**

It seems ironic that with all the people Frank could cure, he could not heal Anna; he could only alleviate her pain for short periods-of-time. Although now very frail, she was still as clairvoyant as ever.

"One morning, several men (all cousins) went hunting. One of the men who was due at work later that morning, never returned. There was an extensive search covering hundreds of acres. The missing cousin could not be found.

"Frank André had been treating members of these families and they knew of Mrs. André being psychic. Two of the female relatives consulted her and she told them they would find the missing man in a miner's ditch under a bush.

"Because of heavy snows, the search had to be terminated. It wasn't until several months later that someone found his remains, his clothes, and rifle under a bush. The place was just as Mrs. André had described it." **Anonymous**

"It was while living in San Jose, California that my family became friends with Ernest and Anna who lived nearby. The Andrés moved to San Francisco and later to Mosquito.

"Our family moved to Santa Cruz. Even so, my parents and the Andrés stayed in close touch by writing one another. When my mother began having bad headaches, we would drive all the way to Mosquito from Santa Cruz for her to have a treatment from Frank. No one else was able to help her.

"Then our family moved to Placerville in the early thirties. For many years, my mother made André's shirts and did any mending the family needed done. My father, Lowell West, later became sheriff of Placerville.

For Fair, Impartial Law Enforcement

LOWELL O. WEST

SHERIFF

EL DORADO COUNTY

PRIMARIES AUGUST 25, 1942

"Patients would stop by now and then to give my dad a list of things the Andrés needed brought to them from town. My parents were happy to do so. Frank never charged our family a penny for his medical services. It was always a mutual exchange.

"Let me tell you, ANNA ANDRÉ WAS CLAIRVOYANT. She occasionally had thoughts that were pertinent to a case my father was working on.

"Because the Andrés had no telephone, Anna would often send one of Frank's patients into town with a message to my father. Sometimes she told my father who to look for and where to look.

"One time Anna sent my father an urgent message warning him that on a certain day he should take extra caution in anything he did. She said his life was in serious danger. On the day in question, after attending a Peace Officer's meeting in Folsom, my father had come to Sacramento to take me to dinner.

"Two hours after returning me home, I received a call from someone at Dad's office telling me my father was in the hospital. They said he had cuts and bruises all over his body and was near death. They said that while driving back to his office in Placerville, my dad received word of some cattle-rustling going on.

"From here, the story was never really clear. The FBI was brought in. The agents said either my dad had been stopped by someone along the road in a planned ambush or there had been someone in the back seat of the car from the time we left the restaurant.

"The car had rolled over and then he was either thrown or dragged from the car, severely beaten, and then pushed and kicked down an embankment.

"My dad's ear was ripped from being hit from behind by a blackjack or some other heavy instrument. His badge had the impression of a heel from someone who had kicked him in the chest while he was down.

"The sheriff's office thought it was an ex-convict from Folsom Prison that my father had help convict. My dad did survive and after this, my dad really listened to Anna. He would go there immediately anytime she sent a message to him. Anna was NEVER wrong in anything she told my father or our family." **P. Johnston**

"My grandmother, Bertha Packard, worked for the Goat Doctor doing their cooking and cleaning. I was eight or nine when one day we went to visit her.

"It was hotter than the hinges on you know what. I remember the story she told us about a man who kept coming around trying to buy the property from the Andrés.

"He kept coming back with higher offers until the Goat Doctor's mother finally told him she knew of his having killed a man, and told him to go away and stay away, and he did." **J. Moss**

In 1947, other than their concern for Anna, things were running fairly smooth for the family. Ernest and Anna arranged a party for Frank's 59th birthday.

On this day, as they did for special occasions, the Andre's gave a man they knew a couple of their butchered kid goats to take to his home to cook in a pit in the ground. The man would keep one and return one to Frank. They served potato salad and vegetables along with the barbecued meat.

"Frank always had me bake a cake for their birthdays. I remember him being very generous. I received something like twenty dollars a cake."
L. Beckett-Pearson

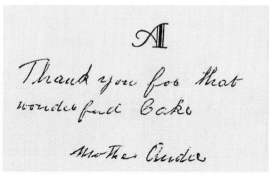

In his later years, Frank would dress up for special occasions. He enjoyed celebrating his birthday with patients and friends. One year, he received a portable electric record player, however there was no electricity to play it.

"I recall seeing a small record player sitting on top of a chest of drawers. It had a bunch of dollar bills sticking out all around from underneath it."

Dr. L.E. Shortes

Frank with birthday cake

Ernest wrote the following poem for Frank's fifty-ninth Birthday.

130

Happy Birthday To You – (1947)

We are glad on this occasion to record the sterling worth
Of our foster son upon the anniversary of his birth.
All his friends, and they are many, we feel certain will agree
That to comfort the afflicted is a precious destiny.

What a boon to have the power to relieve and conquer pain!
Is there any higher calling in the whole of Work's domain?
To release a suffering brother from the clutches of Despair,
Who might otherwise have perished in the cruel Giant's lair;

To bestow on some poor sufferer a more cheerful view of life,
Who perchance had ceased to struggle in the nerve-destroying strife:
This it is to use one's talents freely for the common good
In the spirit of the workman who aspires to Brotherhood.

Yes, his hands are sentient organs, and his fingers apprehend
The location of the lesion, which he follows to the end
That if possible recovery may ensue, and once again
The brother or the sister may obtain relief from pain.

On the question of diplomas, or the Hippocratic Oath,
A record of successful years we may plead in place of both:
In sacroiliac cases he has taken a degree,
And for cures considered hopeless he can claim supremacy.

Everyday you see them coming, young and old and rich and poor,
And whatever their condition they are welcome at the door;
They are met with friendly greetings and the power to console,
With adjustments for the body and suggestions for the soul.

He relies on the Eternal to direct him on his way:
In submission to that Guidance he will never go astray.
In his pathway will be lions, but in that Power Divine,
He is safe, - and may he operate long after fifty-nine.

In 1948, Russell Milham, a Placerville attorney, had pain in his legs and was unable to climb the long flight of stairs to his office. He had to hold on to the rail and pull himself up.

His family physician was unable to help his crippling condition so she referred him to a specialist in Sacramento who was of no help.

When he returned to his physician, she told him, "Go see the Goat Doctor. He'll know what to do."

"Russell and I went out to Frank's place often for treatment. Frank was able to eliminate Russell's pain for a time, but he could not completely cure him.

"He always kept the treatment door shut. No one was to enter while he cared for patients. In one corner of the room was a pile of crutches and metal braces. Frank said, 'Whenever I have a patient with these on, I have them take them off and I dispose of them after they are gone.'

"Something that stands out strong in my memories of him, was when he stopped to talk with someone, he used to hold his hands with his fingers sticking up in the air like surgeons do just after they put on their gloves before surgery. I asked him why he did this, and he said it was to keep his energy strong.

"I remember him as always having a twinkle in his eyes. He never got cross; he was always happy and glad to see everyone.

"I learned a lot from him about the benefits of eating fresh fruits and vegetables. When he told me he had never eaten rhubarb, I baked him a rhubarb pie. He liked it so much, that I then brought him a rhubarb plant. He was so tickled he acted like a kid with a new toy.

"We became dear friends and spent many evenings together talking about everything under the sun."

"The first thing he asked Russell to do was to see if he could find anything about some friends he was unable to locate in San Francisco. He said Ernest and Anna had searched for months when he first moved in with them. Never found, Frank finally accepted the fact that they must have been among the 700 people killed in the savage earthquake.

"Frank would not let Russell leave a donation. Likewise, Russell was happy to advise Frank on anything he wanted to know, free-of charge. Russell often talked with Frank about what to do with his money.

"One time while visiting Frank, who was dressed in his usual after work attire of tan-gray work pants and an army-type shirt, he was sitting in a chair with his feet up on a stool. I couldn't help but notice the bottom of his feet looked like the soles on a shoe, the skin was so thick, after so many years of going barefoot.

"Another time there, I remember looking up the hill on the other side of Mosquito Creek where the earth was riddled with holes.

Russell & Gretchen Milham

"Frank told us they were from the mud baths he and Anna used to take. He told us the hills of Mosquito reminded him a lot of where he grew up as a child. Then he began telling us about his younger years and about the political uprisings and famine in his homeland.

"Frank said he was in his early teens when the couple who raised him told him they had found information about his natural parents. They said authorities told them the couple had been killed on the day he was found and that their deaths were simultaneous and highly suspicious. He didn't go into detail but I got the impression their deaths were not accidental." **G. Milham-Desjardin**

Frank told Russell he knew Anna was nearing her last days on earth. Russell advised Frank to take care of his naturalization papers. On February 5, 1948, he was issued a certificate of citizenship from the Superior Court in Placerville.

"I went with Frank as a witness when he filed for naturalization papers. There was no trouble."
O. Beckett

"Frank Macek André was Czechoslovakian from the Balkan region of Europe. He never told anyone of his origin until after he became a citizen."
E. M. Bliss

Anna spent her last year in a wheelchair, on the cot in the treatment room or in bed. With her dark piercing eyes and long straggly white unkempt hair, her appearance grew weirder by the day. She became outwardly fanatic on religion and spent her last days mailing out religious literature all over the United States.

"Anna looked absolutely wild. In her last couple of years, she sent more mean, nasty letters to neighbors than she ever had before, although, she sent me a very nice one."   **L. Beckett-Pearson**

"We went to the Goat Doctor's place August 26th and found his mother had passed away during the night. Dr. André had us take him into Placerville to have someone come take care of her body." **C. Smith**

Anna André helped and healed thousands of people throughout her lifetime, yet her death record lists her occupation as "housewife".

Mountain Democrat - Placerville
After a lingering illness, which she bore with Christian fortitude, Annie Elizabeth André, loving wife of Ernest André and greatly loved mother of Dr. Frank André, sank quietly to rest at the family home in Mosquito District on Saturday, August 25th, 1948.

A natural healer, she worked with her son, Dr. Frank André, in his osteopathic work, diagnosing the cases of many sick people who came to be treated, many from distant parts of the State; and many who can testify to the cures performed by them. Thoroughly honest, if the disease had progressed too far for them to hold out any hope of permanent relief, they would say so.

The best tribute that could be paid Mrs. André is the poem that follows, written by her husband several days before her passing.

Our Mother

I sing of one who came to me
In the shadowy long ago;
Whose penetration holds the key
To what is high and low
In Moral Law; with power to see
To forecast, and to know.

Forever seeking Wisdom's aid
To reach a higher plane,
She struggles onward, unafraid,
Her goal to attain:
A daily glorious crusade
No illness can restrain.

For Pain has been her heritage,
Afflicting night and day:
Increasing with advancing age,
That nothing can gainsay:
A foe that drugs can but assuage,
But cannot drive away.

Strangers consult her every day,
Seeking her sound advice:
She sends them comforted away,
Willing to sacrifice
Her time and her vitality,
Free from a thought of price.

The economic tragedy
That stalks the world today;
This governmental anarchy
The People to betray,

She saw approaching stealthily,
Increasing day by day.

Coming events she apprehends,--
A prophet and a seer:
The cataclysm that impends,
The crisis that is near:
This she imparts unto her friends,
And all who care to hear.

And now with evil overthrown,
Rising above desire,
She comes at last into her own,
To all she may aspire;
And waits to her The Master's Voice:
"My daughter, come up higher!"

Anna was buried in a bronze casket on a hill called Inspiration Point at the André Ranch Cemetery. Frank had a graceful wrought iron fence built around her grave.

"Anna showed Frank where she wanted to be buried. She loved that one spot on the hill."

J.D. Lawson

Inscribed on a small granite tombstone, her epitaph reads:

Annie Elizabeth André,
1865 - 1948
One of God's Children

Ernest and Frank were so grief stricken and depressed after Anna's death they could barely function. Evidently, they wanted to be alone at this time as it is known that no one was there working and everything became dirty and rundown.

"My mother would take food to Frank and Ernest after Anna died. They were like little lost boys. Without her, they seemed to not know what to do from one day to the next and tended to disagree about everything. They needed a woman about and Anna had been such a driving force."   **C. Neilsen**

"We were living in Citrus Heights some time around 1948-49 when my father began suffering with pain due to arthritis. He had heard so many people talking about how great the Goat Doctor was.

"This included members of the Lion's Club and various doctors. Having not been able to get relief after being seen by the local physicians, in desperation my father decided to go see the Goat Doctor.

"The whole family made the winding trip to Mosquito. We children had to wait in the car while my father went into the cabin to be seen by the Goat Doctor.

"There we sat looking at this little old shack with goats roaming all around it. I had to use the bathroom, which in this case was an outhouse.

"It stunk all along the path from the strong stench of goats, even inside the outhouse. I asked my father what the Goat Doctor looked like. He said, 'He has a long white beard and he looks and smells like a goat.'"   **J. Jones**

"The place was really primitive. The rooms in the cabin were dark, smelly, and full of cobwebs."   **S. Regoli**

"After his mother passed away, Dr. André would often say how he missed her and the insight she had. He always gave so much credit to her training. He felt he could not take care of the patients without her."   **R. Maguire**

"Frank was so depressed after Anna's death. He got word to me and said he wanted to give it all up— he didn't feel he could do it alone. He always felt Anna was behind his touch when he helped people.

"When he sent word to me again three weeks later, he said something told him he had to keep on. It took awhile but little by little he got back to it."

P. DeWolfe

"We used to go and clean the old man's room. I'm pretty sure they did keep records in the beginning. I saw numerous volumes of books and tablets and what appeared to be patient records in the closet in Ernest's room.

"My husband and I could only get out there every month or so. We would take the ashes out of the wood stove, take down the cobwebs, and sweep the floors.

"Frank described to me how he felt after Anna's death. He told me that when he came down from the hill where he had buried his mother, he felt he couldn't carry on without her.

"He had taken care of her night and day and was so overly tired and weak he couldn't lift his arms. When he got back to the cabin, the waiting room was full of people.

"He felt he didn't have the ability or the strength to practice. He told the people he was sorry, but he would not be practicing anymore. As the people were leaving, the last person going out the door was a little crippled boy.

"Frank said it just broke his heart. He stopped the boy, saying, 'Come here son, let me take care of you.' Then he asked the other people to come back in telling them, 'I will try.'

"He told me, 'The instant I became willing, my strength came back to me.'

"From then on, he practiced by himself. He often told people, 'If you have the will to tackle something, you will have what it takes to do it.' I have used this myself all my life."   **E. Clark**

"Healing takes place from within. When we move our thoughts away from our self and concentrate good thoughts to others, we begin to heal ourselves."
                    Frank André

Shortly before Anna's death, a young woman was carried into the treatment room on a stretcher. Her name was Carmelita. She had been in a bad accident; her legs and back were severely injured. Considered a hopeless cripple, her husband brought her to the Goat Doctor as a last resort. Frank told them he could help her, but she would have to have daily treatments for some time. The couple brought a

small house trailer and parked it on the Goat Doctor's property. Her husband had to leave her there, as his work was too far away to commute. Each day, with the aid of a wheelchair, Frank and his helper managed to get Carmelita from the trailer to the cabin where she spent the day on the bed in the resting room. Frank treated her throughout the day, between caring for his other patients.

His healing hands brought relief, and within weeks, Carmelita was walking. She had her health back, but was minus a husband. She moved into the guest cottage and made no attempt to go home. She seemed to cause as much controversy and tongue wagging as Frank and Anna had years before.

"Carmelita stayed in the little house a long time. I thought it was a storage shed. She just moved in. I guess she supposedly thought she was taking care of him. After being healed, she just plain camped on Frank's doorstep."   **B. Alexander**

"Carmelita took care of the doctor and dedicated herself to him and his work after he helped her walk again."   **W. Swansborough**

"She was just plain ornery. I thought she was mean to Mr. and Mrs. André."   **I. Meadows**

"Carmelita came to be treated and just stayed. No one seemed to like her."   **P. DeWolfe**

"Carmelita was about five-feet-four inches tall. If she were any shorter, she'd have been square. The first time I ever met her, she was driving a 1946 Ford Coupe. She had had a wreck on the other side of the river. She ran around the curve on the wrong side of the road, hit a car head on, and totaled out her car.

"She had a foul, raspy personality and a vocabulary of a muleskinner and was 'giving him hell' for running into her, when she was right against the ditch on his side of the road.

"A few weeks later, my wife and I stopped to see if Dr. André wanted anything from town. Carmelita had begun to 'bug' Frank.

"He asked us to take her into town to catch a bus. He said she had no business being there with two old men. She was dang near 40 years younger than Frank. So, we wound up taking her to Sacramento because she missed the bus in Placerville. It wasn't three days until she was back again.

"She immediately began working on the doctor to alienate him from his friends and neighbors. Carmelita had designs on Frank from the beginning."

O. Beckett

"I remember seeing Carmelita working hard around the place. She was milking the goats, cleaning the house and assisting the doctor with the patients." **E. Clark**

"I was ten or twelve years of age when my aunt and uncle from Elk Grove came by our house one day to take my mother and me for a little trip. It turned out to be a day I would never forget, a real experience when we went to visit the Goat Doctor.

"I think my uncle heard of him through one of the butcher shops he did business with in buying the hides of animals. These he then resold for the manufacture of purses, belts, and various other such items.

"I can't remember for sure who was seen by the Goat Doctor or for what reason. We got there early, but not early enough to beat the bunch of cars ahead of us.

"After my uncle parked the car, I got out to play. I began talking with a girl, that is, she seemed like a girl, because she played games and even climbed trees with me. Though she later told me she was in her twenties. She and I ended up spending the whole day together. She was really interesting.

"She went into the cabin and made up a lunch for the two of us. It consisted of an apple apiece and cottage cheese.

"She invited me to come along as she herded six or seven goats along with a gray German shepherd dog, up to the top of a hill to graze. When we got to the top of the hill, we climbed a black oak tree.

"Then she showed me the grave where the Goat Doctor's mother was buried. In talking about the mother being buried, she came up with, 'People think we bury money here when we don't.' She said how silly people were to say such things.

"She told me, 'He saved my life and he does so much good. I'm going to donate my life to helping him. I'm never going to leave here so long as he lets me stay.'

"I felt she was utterly devoted to him. I have never met anybody so kind. I felt hers was a love of complete devotion, from gratitude and respect. As young as I was, I felt they did not have sex. I truly believe she worshipped and adored him.

"I left there with the very warm feeling of a wonderful day. It was really a memorable experience."   **G. Hopkins**

"Carmelita's family lived on an orchard ranch outside of the town we lived in. They were hard working, lovely people and highly respected. I'm pretty sure they are Sicilian.

"I went to the Goat Doctor, as did many people in our area. Some made regular pilgrimages to Mosquito each year. Most of them were in desperate need of medical help." **Anonymous**

"Dr. André invited us out to their home for dinner. Carmelita was there, also. She told how she had been crippled and now wanted to 'repay' Dr. André for the miracle of having healed her.

"She offered to help feed the goats, etc. She made herself very useful and seemed to have a plan to work her way into Dr. André's life." **E. Teany**

Chapter Five
1950-1959

The fifties began peacefully enough. Although the men still greatly missed Anna, most of the somberness that had permeated the air for so long had diminished.

Frank was beginning to appreciate Carmelita a little more each day as she adapted to his needs while assisting him with patients in the treatment room.

Ernest, now in his eighties, was enjoying letters and visits from several ladies who shared his interest in writing and poetry. This came about after Gretchen introduced him to members of the Shakespeare Club where he became very popular with the ladies, and was rejuvenated by the attention he received from them.

Ernest Andre

Ernest enjoyed carving letterhead presses for his friends such as this one he used on his letters.

Sometime after Anna's death, Frank had a telephone installed and gave Ernest the job of setting appointments, which he enjoyed and was proud to do.

However, it did not accomplish their objective which was to lessen the amount of traffic along the road. People still came and sat in wait, with or without appointments, and Frank was back to working longer hours. It became more than he could handle.

"I drove out to see him one day in the early fifties. It was late afternoon and cars were lined up ahead and below the cabin. There were about 25 to 30 people standing around. For a quarter of a mile, people were camped in every direction—all over the place, on the hill and some camped in circles.

"All of a sudden, Frank came out of the house barefoot and carrying a bucket. He spoke to no one, just went out and milked the goats.

"After putting the milk bucket in the house, he came back out and said, 'I am done for the day. Come back tomorrow.'

"There was lots of groaning and grumbling. I spoke up and said, 'Can't you see he has no more to give?'

"With that, he turned and pointed his finger at me and said, 'Come in, I want to talk to you. You understand.' From then on we had a close friendship.

"He was very interested in my work and in our mutual understanding of the life forces and 'out-of-body experiences'."   **E. Teany**

One neighboring family took advantage of the many people waiting along the road by converting their home into a restaurant.

"My mom had a kind of a store/cafe in our house. She used to serve sandwiches, cold drinks, and beer. People didn't want to lose their place in line by driving clear into Placerville to eat, so they would come into our place. We had the store for about two and a half years.

"A woman used to come yearly from Wisconsin and would stay in Placerville for a week. She would come here daily to see Frank. When she first came, she was in a wheelchair. The last year she came, she spent the week in our home. When she left, she was walking."   **B. Webster**

Through the years, Frank accepted rides more frequently. Now in his sixties, feeling tired and unwell much of the time he began seeking medical help for himself, and asked friends, neighbors, and patients for rides.

"Often, on my way home from work on Fridays, I would pick Frank up and take him to Placerville. He had a few doctor friends he would visit. I would tell him I would pick him up in the morning if he could stay overnight but he always chose to walk home.

"I think he got medication for himself. He could help other people but he couldn't heal himself."   **A. Boeding**

"My mother's practice was in Placerville and I know Dr. André came to her a few times as a patient."
B. Julier, M.D

"We remember the multitude of cars that were always around lining the roadway. Whenever we traveled over the western part of the country, we always seemed to meet someone who knew of the Goat Doctor.

"My husband's mother taught high school in Placerville and sometimes, when the Goat Doctor had to get to town, he would walk up to their place and ride in with her. The family lived only a half mile away."
W. Swansborough

In 1953, the Internal Revenue Service began an investigation into Frank's practice. In Placerville, the talk was that someone in the medical field had reported him.

On July 8,1955 a lien was filed against the property and he was once again threatened with arrest.

"We met Dr. André in 1947 and got to know him well. When he first had some problems with the IRS, he hired my husband, Norman Kamp, to do his income tax.

"I can remember Norman saying all that the doctor ever deducted for office equipment were two hot water bottles and a few goatskins each year."
E. Kamp

"At one point, André got in trouble over his taxes and the IRS was threatening him with arrest. My father, Sheriff Lowell West, drove into Sacramento to the IRS board and went to bat for him.

"They must have accepted my Dad's explanation, because André never had a problem after that.

"My Dad thought the world of André; he really loved him. André did so much good. My father used to tell everyone, 'Nobody is going to arrest André while I'm around!'"   **P. Johnston**

"I put my back out. Having lived in the area for many years, we had heard of the Goat Doctor. It was in the middle of winter and the roads were frozen. We were his first patients that morning.

"We knocked on the cabin door and his father let us in. He said the doctor was still out caring for the goats. After a short wait, he came into the cabin.

"He took off his jacket and rubber boots and started a quick fire in a tin heater with pine needles and pinecones. It warmed the place surprisingly fast.

"As we had come in before he had his breakfast, he asked that we excuse his getting a bite to eat. He reached over to a nearby shelf where several ears of dry Indian corn lay, picked one up, shucked off the husk, and began chomping on it raw right there, sound effects, and all.

"He had me sit on a low stool, put a pillow between his knee and my back and proceeded to give me a pull. The crackling noise my back made sounded like someone running the keyboard of a piano.

"He fixed my back in that one session. My mother was with me. After he took care of me, she told the doctor she had a pelvic problem.

"André said, 'That's my specialty.'

"He proceeded to give her a treatment that was unusual, but very effective. She had just one treatment and never another problem.

"When I asked how much I owed, Dr. André said, 'I used to ask $3, but I went back to $2 because I had to pay too much in taxes. Besides, if I abuse my gift, God will take it away.'"   **S. Hill**

By this time, Frank and Carmelita's relationship had taken on a more personal appearance. She was working fulltime as his assistant and living in the cabin.

She seemed to cause as much controversy and gossip among patients and neighbors as Frank and Anna did when they first moved to Mosquito. Once again, there were mixed-sentiments—people either liked her or were adamantly against her.

"One time while Frank was giving me a treatment for my neck, we were talking with Frank about his gift of healing.

"Frank said, 'I will never marry, as my mother told me my healing powers would be gone if I did.' I could see the curtains move on the kitchen side of the window. After Carmelita moved into the cabin, she used to stand behind the window listening. I'm sure she overheard him.

"I talked with Carmelita a lot. She intentionally separated from her husband then divorced him to get Frank. I knew when she moved into the house after the divorce she thought she had pulled a fast one. My husband and I both felt she was after Frank's money and land.

"Once she moved in with Frank, she just plain took over. She was really something. She used to walk down the middle of that narrow road, making cars wait until she decided to get out of the way.

"If anyone said anything to her about it, she'd say, 'I'll walk where I please, I pay my taxes!'

"She talked Frank into going places with her in the car. She talked him into going to Reno to the clubs. He went for the dinners and to watch people, but not to gamble.

"That girl came to me one day and said, 'We drove down the hill to Coloma and the brakes didn't hold. I had to run into rocks, road banks and bushes to stop.'

"She laughed hysterically as she said, 'I guess I should have had the brakes fixed.'

"Carmelita laughed again as she told me how she had changed Frank's diet. 'I've got him eating pork chops and steaks fried in bacon grease, fried potatoes and other foods he never had before.'

"Knowing the doctor's diet was vegetables, fruit and kid meat, I said either, 'He shouldn't eat that', or, 'He never eats fried food.' She said, 'Well, he eats them now.'" **G. Milham-Desjardin**

"Carmelita was almost primitive. That's not to say that primitive isn't good, it was simplistic. When she first came, she was in horrible pain.

"She had had an accident that almost destroyed her. Frank helped her and brought her back to life and she was grateful and humble. She began helping him with his patients and did work around the place.

"Whether Frank and Carmelita were sexually involved, I don't know. I always felt theirs was a totally platonic relationship." **C. Neilsen**

"I have a handicapped daughter. She has Cerebral Palsy. My husband and I took her to see Dr. André when she was five in the early fifties.

"She was in a body brace and used crutches. She had no feeling to speak of in her feet. Her legs scissored and she had no sense of balance.

"The Goat Doctor examined her and said she looked like she had been dropped. We adopted her in this condition, so I don't know what caused the cerebral palsy.

"He gave her a treatment and said he could help her, but he would have to see her each day for some time.

"Since my husband had to work and I couldn't take her back and forth, as we lived so far away, we asked if we could rent enough space to put a mobile home on his property so our daughter and I could stay there and she could see him daily.

"It was our heartfelt desire to stay there and have him treat her but he wouldn't allow it and I had to accept it.

"After returning home in Sacramento, we removed her body brace and shoes and rubbed her feet. She complained that the bottom of her feet itched—they never had before.

"The skin color looked more normal and they didn't feel cold. Later that day it dawned on us that her feet itched because of the treatment. She had circulation in them!

"His home was a shanty surrounded by goats and he looked like a recluse, but he was truly gifted. And although we were heartsick we couldn't make arrangements for our daughter, at least we saw his works and knew he was no phony.

"The lady he lived with was named Carmelita. It was through the grapevine that I later heard it was because of her that we couldn't put a mobile home on his acreage."   **V. Hamann**

"Carmelita was there in the house when I was there. I never heard anything negative about her. She was very quiet and seemed very industrious.

"I think she was a wonderful help to him. A man as busy as he was didn't have time to do the cooking, cleaning, and everything that was involved in running the place.

"A lot of people may have had the conception that Carmelita was trying to take advantage of him. I felt they were two people helping one another. He needed her and she needed him."   **D. Dodge**

Things were never the same in the André household after Carmelita moved in. Frank and Ernest's relationship began to suffer. Ernest had always been jealous of the bond between Anna and Frank and the time they spent working together, and had shown his annoyance in a sulking manner. Now, he was envious of the time and attention Frank was giving Carmelita. Ernest hated her and verbally let it be known.

"The air of animosity was so thick whenever the two were in the same room, you could have cut it with a knife.

"If there were problems in the house, it wasn't because of Carmelita. She was filling an empty space and Dad (Ernest) resented her.

"He was too old to handle a young woman in his household—there was no doubt about that! It wasn't that there was something wrong with her; it was just that he was too old to adjust."   **C. Neilsen**

"I know Carmelita didn't treat Ernest badly, but Ernest was full of animosity because of the whole situation. She couldn't have pleased him if she had stood on her head in a corner."   **E. Clark**

Although eight years had passed since her death in 1948, Anna's estate had not been settled. It is not known if Carmelita acted on her own, or on Frank's behalf, when she filed a petition for distribution of Anna's estate on January 13, 1956.

A hearing was set for January 27. The court found the estate ready for distribution and decreed the sole inheritor of Anna André's estate was Ernest F. André.

Due to age and neglect, the cabin was in serious need of repairs. After a harsh winter in 1956, Carmelita and Frank hired local carpenters to take care of renovations.

"As near as I can remember it was the spring of 1957, when I went over to his place to do some work along with another carpenter.

"We installed all new windows, two doors, and some siding. The siding was installed on the addition to the front part of the log house used for his work and sitting room.

"The original house was made of logs with raw linseed oil on them. He and his mother had built it. The fireplace was made out of local rock that was stacked up with mud.

"The patients would wait outside on benches or in their cars. I saw them go in with a cold sweat, in a wheelchair, and walk out and get into their car and leave! People from all over the world came to see him.

"I remember the doctor wore bib overalls, a white T-shirt, was barefoot with a gray-white ponytail. He had about thirty-five or forty goats at the time. Except for a few pets, they were let out to run wild during the day."   **K. Nevins**

The discord between Ernest and Carmelita continued to grow. On several occasions Ernest sought refuge with the Milhams, often staying with them a week at a time. When he returned home, he kept to himself and seldom spoke to anyone other than Frank.

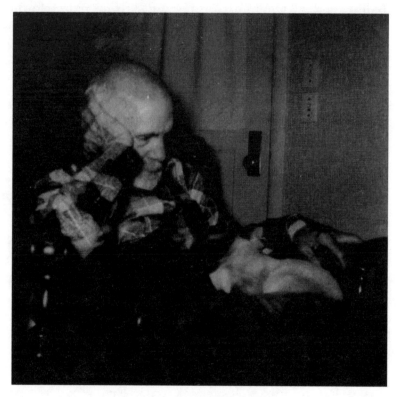

Ernest at the Milhams

"For years we had helped Frank with Dad André. He would sometimes call and ask me to come get the old gent when he wanted him cleaned up. We'd take care of his nails, hair, and trim his goatee.

"Now Dad, himself, was calling me to ask if I would come and take him home with me so he could get away from Carmelita for a few days.

"When I got there, he couldn't wait to get in the car. All the way to our home he would rave about how he couldn't stand her, and how he was afraid of her.

"Each time we picked him up, he was more frightened of Carmelita. He was almost blind. The bathroom was between the kitchen and Ernest's room but he had to feel his way down the stairs to use the outhouse because, other than coming in the back door and going into his room, she didn't want him in the house.

G. Milham-Desjardin

Gretchen

"My gosh, for years I hardly ever saw Ernest, he just stayed in that little back room of his."

A. Neilsen

One day Frank had a long talk with Ernest. He told him how unhappy he was with the way he treated Carmelita. Frank asked him, for all their sakes, to try to get along with her. He said he wanted Carmelita to stay and he intended to marry her.

"Frank said that since Carmelita was a young woman and many people were making remarks, he felt that he should marry her.

"Up to then, he had completely lived a celibate life."

E. Teany

"Carmelita put her foot down and insisted Frank marry her." **G. Milham-Desjardin**

On July 12, 1957, Carmelita's name was added to the deed on property Frank owned. Eight days later, on July 20, 1957, on Frank's 69th birthday, the couple drove to Sparks, Nevada where a Justice of the Peace married them in a double ring ceremony. Carmelita was 31 years of age.

Dr. and Mrs. Frank André (courtesy- David A.)

Mountain Democrat "The bride wore a pink bolero dress with a spray of Lilies of the Valley in her hair. Both wore gold crosses, she around her neck, and he upon his lapel to signify a life of continued Christian service. They had no attendants."

While the couple honeymooned at Bodega Bay for two weeks, Ernest stayed at the cabin and cared for the animals As soon as they returned, he once again called Gretchen and asked if she would come for him. He remained at the Milhams so long Frank became concerned. Ernest missed Frank and wanted to return.

"Not long after Frank and Carmelita married, she got in touch with me and asked if we would take Frank over to the Milhams.

"She said Frank wanted to assure himself that Ernest wasn't being held there against his will. My husband, Frank, and I went there to be sure Ernest was all right."   **E. Clark**

Ernest returned shortly thereafter, but not for long. He was in his nineties and beginning to act senile. He could be intelligent one moment and act like a five-year old the next. He was also taking more than just a little nip now and then. This was something Frank absolutely could not tolerate.

"Many times Frank would send someone into town to get me to help him clean or care for his father. Ernest was getting drunk and would run away.

"He would just start walking until someone would pick him up and take him even as far as Sacramento where he had friends. He loved light switches. They had nothing but kerosene lanterns and I think Ernest wanted some of the conveniences in his later life."   **E. Teany**

"The only time I remember Frank to really get mad and lose his temper was with Ernest because of his drinking."   **G. Milham-Desjardin**

Between giving Carmelita a bad time, his senility, his drinking, and running away, Ernest had really become a problem. After returning from one of his ventures, all hell broke loose.

"One stormy winter night, Frank called and pleaded for me to come quickly and get his dad. He said Ernest and Carmelita had had a big confrontation and that he felt he had had a slight stroke. He said Carmelita had left in a huff and could we try to get there before she got back.

"I can still hear Ernest crying out in fear in the background. I drove out as fast as I could on that rough road to get him.

"When I got there, as I knocked and opened the door, he said, 'Thank God you've come to rescue me from that evil bitch!' But Dad André absolutely refused to go until after the ambulance came and he saw them take Frank away to the hospital. It got there within fifteen minutes of us—around 11:30 p.m.

"He said Carmelita was a devil and couldn't be trusted. He was sure she was out to kill Frank. Frank had a gas stove in his room and Ernest was frightened that she would turn the gas off and then turn it on again unlit.

"He was a real sight! His hair was such a long, tangled, and matted mess. I had to cut his hair short to unravel it. I spent an hour cutting his toenails and fingernails.

"My husband and I carefully lowered the old gentleman into a tub of warm water and bathed the poor soul. I put clean warm clothes on him and fed

him. The shock of it all almost killed him. He was so
upset I gave him a small glass of wine and he calmed
down."   **G. Milham-Desjardin**

Frank did have a mild heart attack. On his release from the
hospital, his doctor told him to take it easy for at least two
to three months. Carmelita put a chain across the driveway
with a notice that Frank was not taking patients because he
was ill.

After resting a couple weeks, it became unbearable for
him to watch the cars drive up, read the sign, and then
slowly drive away. He knew how much they needed him.

Within weeks the chain was removed and the sign on the
twin trees was changed, to indicate he was working half a
day three days a week.

Carmelita removed the smaller treatment table and the
cot from the treatment room, to insure Frank's work would
proceed at a slower pace.

> "After marrying, his wife would only let him work
> during regular hours and nursed him back to health.
> The room where he practiced on patients was just an
> old square room with one chair and a flat table with
> goatskins on it and hanging over the edges.
> "Every time someone needed help, he treated
> them. He almost killed himself from overwork."
> **K. Nevins, Jr.**

Carmelita stayed close by, helping him in every way she
could. In doing so, it changed the atmosphere in the
treatment room. Frank's friends and neighbors resented
her always being there. It took away from their personal
relationship with him.

"The last time I was out to Dr. André was after he had gotten married. Carmelita was right in the room, watching every move that Dr. André made. At that time, I felt uncomfortable. It seemed Dr. André had not been able to help me as he had before. I told my wife that I would never go back."　**G. Bottenberg**

"All of the doctors I knew admired him. He was a real faith healer, but he lost his mystique when he married that woman."　**T. Rulison, M.D.**

Only the family and a few close friends knew what was evolving in the André household. Someone started a rumor that Carmelita had deliberately run Ernest off the property. The animosity against her grew. She was blamed for anything and everything.

"We were good friends of Frank's. Before Carmelita, except for the visiting among the waiting people, it was serenely quiet. The pump from the nearby creek was far enough away to sound like a purr. After they were married, there was always loud music playing. Ernest told me their marriage was the worst thing that ever happened to Frank.

"Before they were married, Frank never charged people he knew. After they were married, his wife increased the amount of donations and charged friends and patients alike."　**E. Tetrault**

"The last time I was there, you had to give Carmelita the money."　**W. Durfey**

"Sometimes we would see Frank up on the road walking to get away from the house. His general attitude was unhappy. He was a gentle person and wouldn't kick her out, but he was definitely a changed man after his marriage." **V. Alexander**

"Everyone said he was doomed when he and Carmelita got together." **N. Eberhardt**

"He married a girl. She got to be domineering. She was nasty to him after their marriage." **M. Clark**

"Everyone around Placerville called Carmelita a gold-digger. That Mexican girl came, stole his near perfect life, and almost destroyed Dad André.

"Frank's Mother had told him he would lose his healing powers if he married and sure enough he soon did." **G. Milham-Desjardin**

"The worst thing going for him was his wife." **S. Coburn**

"There were a lot of negative thinking people in Placerville and they thought what they wanted. They really gave Carmelita a bad time. But those of us who loved him were glad he had Carmelita when he needed her the most. She just loved him." **C. Neilsen**

Because of Ernest's advancing age and signs of senility, Frank and Carmelita became concerned about their rights to the property. They also worried about his very life when he accepted rides from strangers when off on a bender.

Within months of their marriage, while Ernest was still at the Milhams, Carmelita and Frank hired William R. Mitchell, a Modesto attorney, to file a petition for guardianship of Ernest and his estate. Claiming he was infirm and partially blind, they wanted to have him declared incompetent in caring for his own personal business.

On the twenty-first day of November 1957, notice was given that a court date was set for Friday, December 6. Sheriff E.Carlson set out on the twenty-first to serve Ernest a summons to that effect, but he was no longer at the Milham's house and could not be located.

A *Return on Summons Where Defendant Cannot be Found* was filed at the El Dorado County Sheriff's Office.

Ernest was found and served the summons on November 25th at an address in Folsom, approximately 30 to 35 miles away, where he had moved on the 22nd.

On December 4, Carmelita called Russell Milham, Frank's old friend, who now represented Ernest as his attorney. During their conversation, Carmelita stated she and Frank were proceeding no further with the hearing of guardianship. Milham went to the home in Folsom where Ernest was now staying and informed him the matter had been dropped.

However, the next day Milham received a call from the owner of the property where Ernest was staying. The woman told him that Carmelita arrived at her home and remained there talking to Ernest for two hours.

On leaving, Carmelita told the lady that the guardianship hearing **would** be held on Friday, December 6, as originally scheduled. Carmelita was driving a new 1958 Chevrolet station wagon.

Russell Milham requested a continuance for the hearing. He stated, in his opinion, Ernest André was wholly competent and believed that there were good and sufficient grounds for refusing the granting of the guardianship.

On December 11, Milham delivered to Frank and Carmelita's attorney an Answer to the Petition for Guardianship.

In the answer, Ernest admitted that Frank and Carmelita were husband and wife, and that they were not related to him. He stated that he and Anna had taken Francis Macek into their home to live when Francis was 20 years of age, and that he had resided as a member of the family ever since.

Ernest stated he was 92 years old, physically infirmed and that his only impairments were in his hearing and eyesight, together with some inability to walk briskly, and that insofar as his physical well-being was concerned, he had been entirely self-reliant until about November 30, 1957.

He said he procured his own wood for fuel and heating, attended to his own stove, cooked his own meals, made his own bed, and took care of his own physical needs, except for not being able to bathe without assistance. This, he had difficulty in because there were no facilities in the portion of his living quarters in the cabin. He denied he was unable to handle his own affairs.

Ernest alleged he was the owner of real property consisting of a life estate in 200 acres in Mosquito. In addition, he had a bank account; however, Ernest alleged that without his permission or consent, Frank withdrew all of the money from the account.

He claimed that he did not need a guardian to care for his person or his estate. He, being the sole owner of the estate, did not desire to make any change or alteration in the occupancy of the premises, which were occupied by Frank and Carmelita André.

Ernest said he always considered Frank an immediate member of his family, although Frank was never adopted legally. He stated there was no discord between himself and Frank until Carmelita moved into the house.

Ernest had many friends and told the judge he feared that if guardianship proceedings were instituted, he would be denied their visits.

The matter was set-aside for almost a month, to await the judge's ruling. The new court date was January 7, 1958.

During this interim, J.J. Brown, a news reporter for the Sacramento Bee, received a call from friends telling him of their experience on visiting the Goat Doctor.

The wife, in agony for months with severe back pain, received treatment from two doctors, with no positive results. The second doctor told her the only way to correct her problem would be through difficult, risky, and expensive surgery. The woman hated being doped-up on painkillers, yet, was in constant pain when not on medication and was deathly afraid of surgery.

The young couple told Jim when they first heard about the man in the mountains who raised goats for a living and healed people on the side they thought it sounded bizarre.

However, because the woman's fear of surgery was so great, she and her husband decided they would at least go to him and see what he had to say.

They were a very happy and thankful couple when they returned from the mountains and could not wait to tell Jim about their adventure; giving an overall picture of the place and animals and to tell of the woman's complete cure within a few minute of painless manipulation.

Jim found their tale very interesting and decided to check out the Goat Doctor for a story. He called the André residence requesting an interview with Frank.

The following appeared in print on December 26, 1957:

The Sacramento Bee

By James J. Brown   Photos by Leo Neibuaur

A Legend Is Explained; Goat Doctor Of Sierra Tells Of His Life, Work

LEGENDARY—The Goat Doctor of the Sierra, Francis André, holds a kid from his herd of goats. He is dressed in his usual attire, loose fitting denim coveralls. Rays of sun glisten in his long white hair. He has piercing eyes, almost hypnotic, yet kind.

"This is the story of a living legend—the Goat Doctor of the Sierra, as he is known to thousands who have never seen him and to still other thousands who have sought his ministrations over a quarter of a century.

"His career has given rise to countless stories of remarkable healing powers.

"Word of him has drawn ailing visitors from throughout the country and abroad, patients seeking cures for everything from cancer to alcoholism.

A Medical Controversy

"He has sparked medical controversy—including an attempt years ago by the state medical board to halt his work—and he has won the admiration of some medical men for his apparent successes.

"But despite the widespread stories about this extraordinary figure, he has remained a man of mystery to all but a small group of intimates.

"This aura is heightened by the out of the way seclusion of his mountain cabin, in the craggy hills, dense with pine, eight miles north of Placerville, El Dorado County.

"A narrow county road follows a tortuous winding course, skimming the high crests of two ridges and plunging deep into vaulted granite canyons carved by the upper forks of the American River.

Enigma Grows

"And the Goat Doctor's appearance enhances the intriguing enigma: Barefoot, in loose-fitting cotton coveralls, he has a long white mane of hair, worn shoulder length like a Biblical patriarch.

"His eyes—the most arresting feature—are brown, his gaze almost hypnotically direct, piercing, yet gentle, kindly. He is in his 60's but looks much younger.

Who Is He?

"Who is he? What is his story?

"Until now, he has shunned publicity resolutely, would not talk to newsmen. Now he has agreed to the publication of his story for the first time because of the happy occasion of his recent marriage.

"His real name is Francis Xavier Machek but the legal name he uses is Francis André.

"He was born in Vienna, moved with his parents to Czechoslovakia, where they died when he was 6 years old.

"Relatives arranged for his immigration to the United States. He lived in San Francisco with family friends until his early teens when he got a job on a vegetable wagon and became self-supporting.

"It was at that time he met the woman who was to make the profound change in his life—Anna Elizabeth André, a clairvoyant who claimed wondrous intuitive powers and who, with her husband, Ernest, a poet and soldier of fortune, adopted the young Machek.

"From them he took his present legal name. The name Goat Doctor stems from the herd of goats he has kept for years.

A Natural Skill

"'She was a great natural diagnostician,' André says of her. 'She it was who discovered in me my gifts of intuitive powers and taught me most of what I know.'

"Mrs. André died eight years ago. Her husband, André's foster father, now 91 years old, still lives with the goat doctor.

"As a boy, André was in poor health and as his condition worsened, his foster parents took him some 40 years ago to the cabin he still inhabits.

"'My mother knew there was only one thing to do for my condition,' he says. 'That was to get out in the hills and let God's healing powers work on me. After we came here, I began to recover.'"

'The Wild Man'

"'In the first few years, I went around barefoot and naked except for a loincloth. In those days—imagine—people around here called me 'the wild man'!

"'I let my hair grow long because it's a conductor of electricity. If you cut it, it diminishes that power. It conducts the electricity from the air.'

"It was this back to nature therapy, he is convinced, which saved his life.

"'Barefooted—don't forget that,' he adds. 'You contact the soil directly and get the health giving powers of the good earth.'

"It was his foster mother who began the work of healing which the Goat Doctor has carried on, at first with her and since her death alone.

"'She developed my gifts,' he says. 'I've had no formal instructions or taken any training. I'm not a licensed chiropractor, as many people seem to think.

"'The only license I have is the license from above—the gift that was given to me.'"

State Tried to Halt

"The state medical board tried to halt him in those early years.

"'They fought me, but I just ignored them and went on healing people,' he recalls. 'Now, many of the medical doctors send their patients to me—always the worst cases no one can do anything about. Take him to the Goat Doctor they say'.

"'I don't mind being called the Goat Doctor. I'm proud of my goats. Their milk and natural foods like fresh grown fruits and vegetables are the healthiest things one can eat.'

Opinions Vary

"Medical opinion about the goat doctor varies. Some physicians regard him as nothing more than a self-taught chiropractor. Others this writer has talked to say he has achieved surprising success in certain cases.

"Many of them, however, regard these as psychosomatic cures—the power of mind over body—in which André's ministrations were achieved more through the power of suggestion than actual treatment.

"The bulk of his patients, however, are patients with back trouble.

"Testimonials to the Goat Doctor come from all sides. In Placerville, derogatory comments about him most often provoke an angry defense. Newcomers to Superior California sooner or later hear about him.

"His patients have included prominent business and professional men, by their own word—albeit some a little shamefacedly—and these, too, have mostly praise.

Pretends to Heal None

"'I don't pretend to heal everyone,' says André in his own appraisal of himself.

"'Many who come to me I cannot help. I don't claim to cure cancer or diseases which require medical treatment. I tell them to see their doctor. My work, my treatment, is mostly a form of chiropractic adjustment, certainly.

"'A difference is that I will work closer in the pelvic region than most.'

"This, in general, is borne out by patients this writer has talked to. Several would-be patients report André told them frankly he could not help them, referred them to their family doctors.

"André does, however, claim the unusual gift of an intuitive, or sixth sense, which enables him, simply by laying his hands on a patient, to diagnose the exact nature of the ailment.

"'It is a gift from God,' he says. 'I don't pretend to understand it. I just try to use it as He would want me to, to heal.'

Thousands of ailing persons, hopeful of healing, have gone to the Goat Doctor's rough timbered cabin in the hills eight miles north of Placerville, El Dorado County.

Cabin Above Ravine

"Andrés' rustic, rough timbered mountain home, a dark brown roomy cabin, stands on a slanted table of land above a ravine and running brook, surrounded by towering firs and pines.

"His goat clamber the steep paths around the place, nibbling rich green mountain grass.

"All day long, scores of visitors wait outside the cabin in a clearing, their cars—ornate and dilapidated, old and new—crowding the roadside. The patients are called in on a first-come first-serve basis and the fee is a flat $3 to all.

"For the last five years his barefooted assistant has been energetic, raven haired

He is proud of his goat herd, which roams the steep slopes about the cabin, nibbling on green mountain grass.

Carmelita Munoz, who says the Goat Doctor cured her of a crippling condition, became his bride in July.
Bee Photos by Leo Neibaur

Carmelita who dedicated her life to the Goat Doctor after he cured what she says was considered a hopelessly crippling condition of the legs and back.

"Then, on July 20, Carmelita and André, a lifelong bachelor, were married in a double-ring ceremony before a Sparks, Nev. Justice of the peace.

"I think that is why he agreed to a news story now," says Carmelita. 'We are so happy and because of the news of our marriage has come out in so many papers, we thought this would be a good time for you to print the doctor's life story.'"

Frank's statement to J. J. Brown that he had no formal instruction or training was confusing because he told many people he had studied at a chiropractic college and with Dr.

Pinneo. To people who were closer to him, he stated he adhered to Anna's teachings and that which he had taught himself.

He did however receive a license **after** his story appeared in the Sacramento Bee.

A local chiropractor took his ailing daughter to Frank and confessed to him that he and two other doctors had not been able to correct the girl's back problem.

With the father watching his every move, Frank gave an adjustment which appeared no different than what he himself and the other doctors had done, yet within minutes the girl was all smiles and walking. She was miraculously well! The man was dumbfounded.

The chiropractor was so in awe of the healer that he went to the Chiropractic Board and insisted they let Frank take a written examination. Finally, Frank André had the license he had coveted for so many years!

> "Dr. André did take a chiropractic exam. He passed without any problem. He finally got approval from the Chiropractor Association." **B. Waggersman**

> "I know for a fact Frank did get his Chiropractic license." **E. Kamp**

Jim Brown's article not only gave people a glimpse into the life of the Goat Doctor, it brought many more people in search of a cure for themselves and/or their loved ones.

> "Everyone around here had to do their shopping in Placerville. We lived a mile and a half from Frank and to get to town we had to pass his place.
> "It was such an inconvenience for us to have to fight the traffic. On weekdays, it was a major chore and on Friday and Saturday, it was next to

impossible. You cannot believe the thousands of people who came to him!"
C. Neilsen

"It was a couple of days before Christmas, I took off for Mosquito in hopes of giving my good friend, Frank, a pair of slippers I had bought as a Christmas present for him. Having always seen him barefoot or in sandals, I thought he didn't have enough money to buy shoes.

"After half a day of sitting in a cold car waiting in the inevitable line of cars, with the wind and rain loudly swirling all about, I decided to go home. The trip was dangerous enough, without driving in a storm to boot!

"A couple of weeks later, I made the trip again, still wanting to give Frank the slippers. The road was even more lined with cars than the time before. So again, I turned back and headed for home."
D. Thompsen

"We had a soda fountain shop in Georgetown in the late 50's. I had thrown my back out and was in terrible pain. The owner of the Georgetown Hotel, where we were living, told me he was going to take me to a doctor who was sure to fix my back.

"Well, I want you to know I took a nice long bath and got myself all dolled up. I was dressed in my very best dress with my hair styled just so, with nary a hair out of place.

"I mean, I WAS GOING TO THE DOCTOR'S. Little did I know I would end up sitting on the side of a dirt hill for several hours, waiting my turn, along with nine hundred other people.

"He was worth the wait! Within a few minutes, I was standing up straight and walking without pain. Not only that, but I stayed that way!

"This was remarkable considering the fact that I had never had good posture. I was what you might call a sloucher. Not any more! The man was remarkable!"
L. Wagner

"I was a mechanic with chronic back pain. He helped me a lot. I'd have to spend all day waiting. Finally, there was no way to get to see him, so I quit going."
F. Darrington

On January 7, 1958, the day of the guardianship hearing, the judge ruled Ernest was not incompetent and was not incapable of managing his property or taking care of himself to the extent that the appointment of a guardian or conservator of either his person or of his estate be appointed.

Foster Dad, 92, Bests Goat Doctor In Court
McClatchy Newspaper Services

PLACERVILLE, El Dorado Co.—Francis Andre, widely known as the Goat Doctor of the Sierra, and his wife, Carmelita, have been defeated in a legal move to have his foster father, Ernest Frank Andre, 92, declared incompetent. A petition by the couple to obtain the guardianship of the elder Andre was denied by Superior Judge Robert E. Roberts following a hearing yesterday.

They claimed he is infirm and partly blind. He countered by admitting he is 92 years of age but denying he is unable to handle his own affairs. He stated there was no discord between himself and Francis until Carmelita joined the household.

The judge ruled Ernest competent, but added, with such discord now in the André's home and with Ernest in such bad physical shape due to neglect, he should not return to the cabin and could stay at the home of his good friends

Russell and Gretchen Milham, until a suitable nursing home could be found for him.

"I represented Frank Andre and his wife. I felt bad losing—it was my first case in that field. I was a real novice! If I had it to do over today, I know I could win. I remember Frank André sitting in court. He was a quiet, gentle-speaking man. It was obvious his wife was running the show."   **W.R. Mitchell**

"The trial against Ernest was all Carmelita's doings—she was just plain greedy."
                                    G. Milham-Desjardin

In March, Ernest filed a quitclaim to his rights of a portion of the property to Frank and Carmelita for consideration of less than one hundred dollars.

The trial and added workload was too much for Frank; he became exhausted and his health continued to fail.

"Frank and Carmelita came to my home in Sacramento and stayed overnight on a couple of occasions. I'm pretty sure they were in the area for medical reasons. Frank didn't sleep on a regular bed. He said he was used to sleeping on a board with a thin pad on it, so he slept on the floor."   **E. Clark**

"Several months had passed when I decided to give one more try to give Frank his Christmas slippers, only to find he had suffered a heart attack and could see no one."   **D. Thompsen**

Frank's doctor warned it was imperative for him to rest a few months. Carmelita put the chain back across the road and posted a 'KEEP OUT' sign next to it. This stopped most people from coming to the door, but there were always those who thought it could not possibly apply to them—they did not realize how sick he was.

In trying to gain some peace and rest for her husband, Carmelita took a stand and said, "go away" to everyone who came near the door.

When someone called by phone asking to speak with him, her usual response was an abrupt, "He can't talk to you now" or "He doesn't want to talk to you!" Seldom did she bother to say good-bye before slamming down the receiver.

"I studied under Frank and he and I became good friends. I knew him for years. When I heard he was sick, I called and asked Carmelita if I could come for a visit. I called again from Placerville to make sure it was still all right.

"She said that would be fine, but when I got there, she shut the door in my face and said he couldn't see anyone. I wish now that I had insisted on seeing him." **Dr. G. Windmiller**

"He was my friend and I wanted to see if there was anything I could do to help. But Carmelita said he didn't want to see me.

"From that day to this I strongly regret I didn't demand to see him. I just don't believe he said it." **P. Burns**

"The last time we called, we were talking to Frank. We could hear Carmelita yelling, 'No, they're not coming over!' She ruined him and shortened his life." **E. Tetrault**

"He married late in life. His wife put a stop to his work, saying he was very tired and it was time for him to rest.

"I never saw him after he married. I understand she wouldn't let people in to see him."　　**D. Radon**

"Carmelita took good care of Frank, especially when he was sick. She was different and perhaps she could have been more tactful, but some people don't know when to give up, and there were so many bothering them."　　**C. Neilsen**

"After his marriage, I went out and the doctor worked on me, but I felt it wasn't the same. Another time I had to have someone drive me out to see him.

"Carmelita told me the doctor wasn't there and for me not to wait. I was sure I had seen Dr. André in the large garden when we drove up, but he crouched down behind the plants."　　**R. Gust**

During the winter of 1958, Frank suffered another heart attack and once again hospitalized. He could not stand being in the hospital and within days, against his doctor's advice, he insisted Carmelite take him home. It was in the treatment room of his cabin that Francis Macek André lived out the last few weeks of his life before his death on January 16, 1959.

"I was called from the hospital and asked to bring Frank's dad to him. We had to help Ernest up to Frank's room. They had quite a confab and buried their animosities.

"Soon after he went home. We didn't like that she was there, but there was nothing we could do about it. He asked to be put in the treatment room. This was when the Goat Doctor closed the door on his unhappy marriage and died."   **G. Milham-Desjardin**

"After my Aunt Carmelita and Uncle Frank were married, we lived with them for close to a year. They were very loving to one another.

"I remember him giving me a box of pears to hand out to people waiting to be seen. I used to get five cents a pear.

"I used to walk with Uncle Frank to his mother's grave. He always kept it free from weeds. He told me how much he loved and missed his Mumsy Dear. He talked a lot about her.

"I remember his telling me more than once. 'If you ever get lost, be sure to go down hill'.

"There were two beds in the treatment room. Uncle Frank was laying in the hospital bed and I in a regular bed. A very strange thing happened the night he died. All of a sudden, a silhouette appeared on the wall. It looked like the shadow of a man moving across the room. My Uncle Frank got very upset and Aunt Carmelita came in and calmed him down.

"When he seemed all settled, she went out of the room. Uncle Frank started coughing and making noises. Then, he let out a cry and died.

"The goats came right up close to the house and pretty much surrounded it. They stretched their necks as though trying to peek through the windows and began bleating real loud! Then they hung their heads low and wandered up the hill."   **D. Pitts**

Goat Doctor Dies; Final Rites Will Be Monday

1-16-59

Picture on page A12
McClatchy Newspapers Service

PLACERVILLE, El Dorado Co.—Francis André, known as the Goat Doctor by the thousands who beat a path to his door to receive his ministrations during the last quarter

---

Frank M. Andre, 70, famed 'goat doctor' dies in mountain home

Following funeral services Monday afternoon at Memory Chapel, with Rev. Richard E Penaluna officiating, Frank M

NEWS SATURDAY, JANUARY 17, 1959

Final Rites For Goat Doctor Will Be Conducted Monday

PLACERVILLE, El Dorado Co.—Francis Andre, known as the Goat Doctor by the thousands who beat a path to his door to receive his ministrations during the last quarter of a century, will be buried Monday in the family cemetery

---

Funeral For Goat Doctor Will Be Held Monday

Continued from page 1
well being through natural health therapy.

His foster mother began the work of healing which the Goat Doctor carried on, at

---

150 Attend Funeral For Goat Doctor

PLACERVILLE, El Dorado Co. — One hundred and fifty persons attended funeral services conducted for Francis M. Andre, widely known as the Goat Doctor.

The services were held yesterday in the Memory Chapel here with neighbors, friends and patients filling the chapel and standing in the corridor.

The Rev. Richard E. Penaluna of the Federated Church officiated at the simple service, after which the funeral cortege proceeded to the family cemetery at Andre's home place in the Mosquito district, eight miles northeast of here.

Andre, who gained the name of the Goat Doctor from the herd of goats which roamed the place and who gained fame for his healing powers which he attributed to an intuitive gift, died Friday in his home.

She developed my said in an interv 957. "I've had no form truction or taken an ng I'm not a license ractor as many peop think.

"The only license I license from abo ft that was given to Andre, who wore l ng overalls, went t nd with a long whit f hair resembled a atriarch, became a f controversy as his on for healing spread In the early years th edical board tried s practice.

He served his patien rst come first serve nd the fee was a all.

Not All Helped

"I don't pretend t eryone," Andre said terview.

"Many who come t nnot help. I don't c re cancer or disease quire medical treatn ll them to see thei r."

He claimed, howeve usual gift of intuit xth sense.

"It is a gift from Go ated "I don't pret

Goat Doctor Dies In Home After Illness

McClatchy Newspapers Service

Picture on page D2.

PLACERVILLE, El Dorado Co. — Francis Andre, known as the Goat Doctor to thousands who sought his ministrations during the last 25 or more years, died shortly before noon today.

Death came to him in his home 15 miles northeast of Placerville where he received his patients and where he gained the name, Goat Doctor, from the herd of goats he kept.

McClatchy Newspapers Service

"Francis André, known as the Goat Doctor by the thousands who beat a path to his door, to receive his ministrations during the last quarter of a century, will be buried Monday in the family cemetery on his home place in the Sierra.

"Funeral services for the 70-year-old self-taught practitioner, who died yesterday in his home, will be held at 2pm Monday in the Memory Chapel here.

"He suffered a heart attack several weeks ago and had been advised by his physician to refrain from work for three months.

"During his career, it is estimated he treated as many as 100,000 persons, who traveled to his home from throughout California, virtually all the states and from as far as Alaska."

On viewing Frank in the chapel, people were surprised at the incongruous sight of their country friend clothed in a black silk suit with a wide red satin sash across his chest from shoulder to waist.

The room filled to capacity, while hundreds of other people waited outdoors in their cars to honor him, by following in the funeral procession as it crossed the highway and up the ever-winding road through the forest to his burial site.

"The streets were lined for blocks with literally hundreds of parked cars waiting to follow in the funeral procession. His funeral caused the biggest bottleneck Placerville has ever had."   **R. Weichold**

"Frank was to be buried in the family plot way back up on the edge of their land. My husband and I drove up but the traffic was so thick with cars, we stopped short of the burial ground and turned around and went home."   **G. Milham-Desjardin**

"The procession had to cross the main highway from San Francisco to Lake Tahoe. The road had to be closed for a good two hours and the traffic was backed up for miles." **P. Johnston**

Frank was laid to rest at the André Family Cemetery next to his beloved foster mother Anna.

Francis Macek Andre
1888 – 1959

One of God's Disciples

Dedicated His Life to Mankind

Ernest paid homage to his son with the following poem.

DOCTOR ANDRE'

He sought no entry in the race
For envied wealth, for power or place;
But strove towards a higher goal:
The freedom of the Soul.

With her who labored by his side:
His mother, mentor, friend and guide
He dwelt apart and built a shrine
For God and Life Divine.

In visions from the Source of All
He saw a Light and heard a Call
That took him from a world of strife
To teach the Laws of Life.

Upon his brow for all to see
The signet of integrity
Is manifest and in his eye
The light of chastity.

Dowered beyond the common man,
He might have ruled or led the van,
But chose to walk the Narrow Way
And serve from day to day.

Like to the Good Samaritan,
He comforted his brother-man;
Bound up his wounds with hands that blessed,
And lulled the soul to rest.

With hands that never sought in vain
To find the hidden seat of pain,
He ministered to rich and poor
And kept an open door!

No task too hard, no day too long;
He bore each burden with a song'
Nor slander's lies, nor envy's wrath
Could turn him from his path.

In sterile sects and barren creeds,
In war of words and dearth of deeds,
He trusted not; but prayed to find
A way to help mankind.

And as the years rolled by he saw
In part the meaning of the Law
That all the Host of Heaven obey —
That will not pass away!

Secure in Him who cannot fail,
He waits the lifting of the veil
To where, with those who won renown,
His name is written down.

by Ernest F. Andre, *Father*

Upon Frank's death, there were bank accounts in Dixon, Sacramento, Folsom, Placerville, and Reno, Nevada. There were two Certificates of Savings totaling $4,110.36, five savings accounts totaling $47,274.91 and 38 United States Savings bonds purchased between November, 1957 to August, 1958 with face values of $12,825.00. The real property appraised at $13,500,00.

Goat Doctor
Estate Is Set
At $74,541

2-28-59

McClatchy Newspapers Service

PLACERVILLE, El Dorado Co.—Francis M. Andre, self taught practitioner who was widely known as the Goat Doctor because of the herds of goats he kept, left an estate of $74,541.

The total is shown in an inventory and appraisal filed by Don Goodrich, state inheritance tax appraiser. He lists the estate as including two parcels of El Dorado County real estate valued at $13,500, various stocks and several bank acounts, all held in joint tenancy.

The interest of the widow, Carmelita M., is listed as $68,996 and that of Felicia Diaz, a sister in law, at $5,545.

Andre died January 16th at the age of 70. More than 40 years earlier he had moved to the Mosquito district for health reasons.

"We lived close by the Andrés and I got to know Carmelita pretty well.

"I'll never forget one day when she came over with a little white donkey in her car for us to see.

"I'm not sure if in the beginning she married him out of gratefulness or that he married her because he wanted to have someone to leave his inheritance to.

"I do know she loved him.

"You have only one great love in your life and I know he was hers."

L. Nelson

Frank's friends were hurt when they were not able to visit him in his final days. Several told of the guilt they feel to this day, wondering if they let him down by being respectful of his wife's wishes.

The few friends Carmelita had were far out numbered by people who just plain worshiped Frank Andre' and blamed her for taking him from them and the hostility against her grew at the speed of a lynching mob.

"For the last ten years of Frank's life, everyone around here stayed away in droves. No one could stand Carmelita.

"You know, he was revered by a lot of folks. After he died, people really gave her a bad time. A lot of people just have to blame someone when something happens that they can't accept." **L. Beckett-Pearson**

"When they lost the Goat Doctor, people were mad. They were really 'up-in-arms' about it. He was revered. He had saved so many from pain. I, for one, feel she hastened his death.

"After Frank died, she just let his goats roam wild."   **G. Milham-Desjardin**

"He had all the symptoms of arsenic poisoning and I, for one, feel she did away with him." **Annonymous**

"There was a terrible amount of animosity against her. A lot of people felt Carmelita took Frank away from them and resented her for it. I feel she was bad-mouthed and treated unjustly. She was trying to keep Frank alive. A lot of people hated and criticized Carmelita, but no one else was there when Frank truly needed help. The place was going to ruin, as was his health.

"Carmelita loved him. She once called me in Sacramento and asked me to bring him five-dozen red roses and a pair of silk pajamas.

"I will stand up for her anytime—I tell you this even though I had been named in Frank's will before Carmelita came along."   **E. Clark**

After Frank's death, people sneaking onto the property day and night besieged Carmelita. Some came to dig for the money they heard he had buried. Troublemakers came on the property to harass her. Then, there were those who thought the land to be holy and just wanted to walk on it.

It all became too much for Carmelita. She began yelling at anyone who so much as looked as though they might be coming onto the property.

"One day, while driving past the property, I was noticing how tall the corn in her garden was. All of a sudden, Carmelita came running, waving a gun yelling she was going to shoot me if I ever drove slow past her house again!"   **Anonymous**

"I got to know Carmelita. She was a very healthy, domineering, and obnoxious person. She made it clear to anybody who came near the property, if they didn't keep moving, she'd blow their heads off with a rifle."   **B. Scott**

"It was a hot summer day and my friends and I were taking a shortcut across the André place. There was this one spot in the creek that was a little deeper then the rest and we decided to go in. We got right close to it when Carmelita jumped out from behind a bush with rifle, scaring the be-jeevous out of us. She chased us clear to the road, all the while yelling she would shoot us if we ever came near her property again."   **S. Arnold**

"Sometimes she would sit in her car, parked behind the goat shed and if anyone went past the place too slow, she'd take off chasing them with her car."   **D. Brown**

On March 23, 1959, two months after Frank's death, Carmelita, awakened by smoke.

Goat Doctor's Widow, Kin Flee Blaze In Home

McClatchy Newspapers Service

PLACERVILLE, El Dorado Co. — Fire of undetermined origin early today destroyed the Mosquito district home of Mrs. Carmelita Andre, widow of Francis who was widely known as the Goat Doctor.

The loss, including furnishing and personal belongings, was estimated at $10,000.

State forest fire fighting crews reported Mrs. Andre was asleep when smoke apparently awakened her. She got two nephews out of the house and then leaped through a window.

Mrs. Andre suffered cuts on an arm and was taken to a Placerville hospital by J. D. Lawson, a logger.

Neighbors saved Mrs. Andre's car by rolling it from the garage.

"The newspaper got it all mixed up. This is the way it happened: It was around seven in the morning, I was on my way to work when I caught sight of the Goat Doctor's old cabin on fire.

"Then, a little farther down the road I saw Carmelita. She was up near the barn. She had tied a cloth around her arm for a tourniquet. Her young niece and nephew were walking along the road with her.

"When she saw me she said, 'Oh J.D., please help me. I've been trying to get someone to stop but nobody will help me. They all hate me.'

"I got her and the niece into the front seat of my truck and the boy into the back. Carmelita had severe gashes to the underside of her arm from the shoulder to the elbow area.

"She was bleeding profusely. Blood was running down her arm and onto the seat. The foam in the seat cushion soaked it up like a sponge. Carmelita kept telling the girl to make the tourniquet tighter.

"On the drive to the hospital in Placerville, Carmelita told me she and the children had gotten safely out of the house. She then saw her purse inside on a table near the window. She received her injuries when she shoved her fist through a window in an effort to reach the purse. By the time I got her to the hospital, she was turning white. The doctor said she was very near to death.

"Carmelita was very appreciative of my taking her to the hospital. She kept trying to buy me new seat covers for my truck. I told her that wasn't at all necessary.

"Before the fire, I had asked about buying a small house trailer she had on the property. When I wouldn't accept the seat covers, she insisted on giving me the trailer. She said, 'I want you to have it. You saved my life.' It was real nice of her to give it to me. I just wished I could have gotten it before the goats had eaten up the insides!" **J.D. Lawson**

"My husband was a deputy sheriff in Placerville at the time. He said he and everyone in the sheriff's office thought the fire was arson." **V. Fancher**

"There has never been a doubt in my mind that the fire was anything but arson. She had so many enemies." **G. Milham-Desjardin**

"That old house was a firetrap. My goodness, a coal could have popped out of the kitchen stove and started the fire.

"Our family had no thoughts that it was arson. I think the stories about the cabin fire being arson came from the negative group of people." **C. Neilsen**

After treatment for her injuries at the Placerville Sanitarium, Carmelita went for a short stay at her sister's home. When she returned to Mosquito, she moved into the small guest cottage and painted it pink.

"Guest cottage" (courtesy David A.)

At this time, Ernest was living at Mount Danaher Rest Home in nearby Camino. Despite his failing eyesight, he continued writing beautiful verses. Gretchen thought his poems to be outstanding and suggested he have them published. Ernest told her he wrote poetry for the joy of it and did not care to be involved with the business of selling. He allowed Gretchen to buy the poems and she compiled them into book form.

Less than a month after Frank's death, on February 9, 1959, an article appeared in the Sacramento Bee, which included a picture of Ernest with Gretchen by his side at a tea given in his honor by the Shakespeare Club.

CLUB TEA—Mmes. Raymand Geyer, left, president, and Russell Milham, art section chairman, greet Ernest Andre at a tea given in his honor Tuesday by the Shakespeare Club in Placerville. A collection of Andre's poems was published recently in a booklet, Rhymes Of The Mother Lode. Bee Photo

It told of the sale and autographing of his book that contained thirty poems, entitled "Rhymes From The Mother Lode" at Pioneer Book Shop in Placerville.

Sacramento Bee staff reporter V. E. Allen interviewed Ernest on this momentous day. After asking Ernest about his poetry, Allen wrote: "There is a mischievous twinkle in his eyes as he says: 'It's a gift'—and then quickly adds: 'that's what the boy said when he knocked out his brother's front teeth with a two by four.'

"Ernest explained that he always loved reading. Amongst his favorites were Shakespeare, Byron, Hood, Milton, and Longfellow. In a more serious mood, when

Ernest Andre, 92, writes verses on a typewriter more easily than he can with a pen.   Bee Photo

asked about his writing ability, Ernest said, 'It's a gift—the words just come to me. I write on inspiration not on order.'"

Poems of 93-year-old man compiled in new volume

"Ernest became pretty famous after his poetry book was published.

"I can still recall seeing him walking about town looking very distinguished wearing a white suit."

A. Arian

Chapter Six
1960 –1969

Ernest and Gretchen remained close, and a second book containing 101 poems was produced titled *More Rhymes From The Mother Lode.* Gretchen arranged another tea and autograph party for Ernest.   *From Placerville Times below*

STILL WRITING at the age of 95, Ernest Andre had his first book of poetry published two years ago. Now, a second book, a compilation of all his poetry, has been published. Holder of a life membership in the Ina Coolbrith Circle of Poets, a scholarship he won with his poem Dragonfly, Andre is also a member of the Mid-West Federated Chapparral Poets and the California Chapparral Poets. On Sunday from 2 to 4 p.m. Mrs. Gerda Smith and Mrs. Gretchen Milham will co-hostess an autograph tea party for Andre at the rest home at 73 Cottage street in Placerville, where he makes his home. Andre's new book carries a forward by Lillith Lorraine, editor of Flame magazine and past president of International Poets. All friends of Andre and his poems are invited to the autograph party according to the hostess.

Within weeks of the book signing on March 21, 1961, Gretchen was called to Ernest's bedside.

"I remember hurrying home from the Shakespeare Club and how Ernest waited for me to come. He smiled when I bent over to kiss him and then he died.

"He was family to me. I just loved him. He was like my father and I always called him 'Dad'."

G. Milham-Desjardin

Ernest Frank Andre
1865 – 1961
Beloved Husband

The three Andrés were now buried side by side in the André Cemetery on Inspiration Point, with Anna in the middle and Ernest to her right.

Inspiration Point in Andréville

"Most people knew him as the "Goat Doctor's father," and he was content in this title.

"But Ernest of Mosquito held a special talent all his own and the older he grew, the more this talent was appreciated.

"Many men aspire to be poets and many put their hand to the pen, but few men produce lines worthy of merit. Ernest André, in his humble way, wove stories in rhyme that captivated the reader from beginning to end.

"André was a life member of the Ina Coolbrith Circle of Poets, a scholarship he won with his poem, Dragonfly. He was also a member of the Midwest Federated Chaparral Poets and the California Chaparral Poets." **Peg Presba** - Georgetown Gazette

Dragon Fly

I sat beside a stream one day
And watched a dragonfly at play,
And so absorbed he seem'd to be,
I wondered if he noticed me.

But as I marked his airy dance
I thought I caught a subtle glance,
As though he knew I must admire
His radiant wings and eyes of fire.

With perfect poise he rose and fell
As though he wove a magic spell,
And so sweet was the summer air
It seemed to vanish every care.

And then, how swift, away he flew
To other fields and pastures new;
And will me from far off streams
And added virtue to my dreams.

Carmelita continued to live on the André property and in 1962 she had a concrete dam built across Mosquito Creek. It was approximately 190 feet long and 27 feet high, with a 380 feet spillway.

> "As children, my Aunt Carmelita would have my cousins and I come for a few days during the summer. She dammed up the creek so we had a place to swim. I always remember her driving a little blue car with a wheel on the back."   **D. Pitts**

It was also in the early sixties that Carmelita married a logger named Lewis Dick. Called Lewey by his friends and described as a very nice intelligent man, with a speech impediment.

> "My uncle, Lewis used to drive past the Goat Doctor's place on his way to and from work. He'd slow down and talk with them. This was how he came to know Carmelita. After Frank died, my uncle married Carmelita."   **M. Badeker**

> "While at Beeches Mill I worked with Carmelita's husband. He worked on the green chain. He was a well-liked fellow of medium build with blonde hair."   **M. Veerkamp**

> "Carmelita and Lewey Dick got married and then divorced at least three or four times. I don't think they ever really lived together."   **M. Pearson**

> "Lewis Dick had to have more guts than a slaughter-house to marry her. Although, after she had her little boy, she calmed down a little bit. He was an exceptional child, a very bright boy."   **O. Beckett**

"Carmelita and her son lived in the washhouse on the property. I remember when he starting grammar school and what a hard time he had adjusting to the other boys and girls."   **E. Personeni**

"I was born in 1963 and lived with my mother (Carmelita) on the André Ranch for nine and-a-half years. My parents never really lived together. My father, Lewis Dick, lived a short distance, on the other side of the ravine on property he owned before they married.

"Mother and I lived in the little pink house. It was small and had been one level. Somewhere along the line, a couple of bedrooms and a bathroom had been added.

"It caused a big scandal when my mother got involved with Frank. She called him Francis. She told me about the troublemakers who spread rumors that she was a gold digger and only married him for his money. She did not want any of the money!

"My mother is a totally honest person, to a fault. She is also a very generous person. There was a small house across the road that she owned and rented out.

"I remember one time a family with small children couldn't pay their rent and she let them live there a long time rent-free.

"Mother loved Frank very much and always spoke of him in glowing terms. She loved his long hair. She used to tell me that Frank never talked negative about people; he always tried to build them up.

"She liked talking about Frank. Many times, she told me of how he had changed her eating habits by teaching her to eat healthful foods.

"She never took down Frank's heavy rough Levi jacket that was on a hook in the goat barn. It hung there from the last time he wore it.

"Mother said Frank told her he had been found as a toddler wandering alone naked in the snow. He said the couple that found him took good care of him and made sure he was well educated.

"She often used the story of Grandfather André being buried in the earthquake in San Francisco as an example—a lesson of how things could be worse.

"After Frank died, my mother went through years of harassment. One time, a car stopped along the road, a man pointed a rifle at her and fired. She said she felt the current of air as the bullet whizzed by her chin. She knew the people involved, she saw one of the men, but she couldn't prove it.

"It made me sick the first time I saw the suture scars on my mother's arms that she received when the big house (Frank's cabin) burned down. She always felt someone had set fire to the house with her in it.

"She was continually bothered by phone calls. The phone would ring; she would pick it up, listen a moment, and hang it up again. Whether someone was on the line or not, I don't know. She went to the phone company a few times trying to see if they could be traced. Because of this, she hated the phone but wanted to have it in case of an emergency and to call my father.

"Someone was always trying to take advantage of her or finagle something out of her. At different times when mother let people into the house, they managed to sneak out with almost every snapshot she owned. They took plain, simple things like old buckets, lanterns, and tools that attracted them.

"People were forever trespassing on the property, either to harass her, or to steal something. Whenever two or more people came on the property, mother would have me run down and climb up the big old apple tree by the ruins to keep lookout. Sometimes one would come to the door to distract her while the other one would find something to take.

"There was something like a buckboard wagon that had rotted on the side of the house. Antique dealers were always stopping by trying to talk my mother into selling it but she would always run them off. Finally, she just gave it away so they would stop coming to our door.

"My mother loved me very deeply and took excellent care of me. She was very protective of me. Sometimes if a car would slow down or stop on the road, she would tell me to hide behind the house. I got the impression she thought someone was out to get me. Mother lived in fear in Mosquito and you can't imagine how scared I was as a child. For a child to be afraid is one thing, but to see his mother so afraid made it twice as bad. It began to affect her deeply and she had a nervous breakdown.

"One time, when some renters moved out, they left a real nice chrome dinette set; it was much nicer than anything we had in our house. In fact, all we had for an eating table was a board hinged to the wall with two sticks of wood that folded down for legs. Mother had my father put the dinette set in his pickup, drive to the ridge, and dump it.

"However, not before she had taken an axe and chopped the top all to pieces. I asked her why was she doing this and she said, 'It does not belong to us so we cannot use it.'

"There were several boxes of kerosene lamps in the barn. I could never understand why, but she took all the lamps out and threw them into the creek smashing them to pieces.

"There was only one picture, a large oil painting of Frank in our house. My mother told me a famous artist had painted it. One day, she took the painting down and broke it all to bits. She said she destroyed it because somebody had stolen the real one. I'm pretty sure it was the original.

"The only thing left of the big house, that's what we called the Goat Doctor's cabin, was the chimney and a lot of broken glass and melted metal that was scattered all over the place.

Chimney remains [center] and road [right] to guest cottage

"Towards the creek, by the ruins of the big house, was some type of old electrical apparatus, half buried in the ground. It was a big contraption, a large oval tub that looked to be made out of the same material as green insulators.

"There were a few, long things that looked like the inside of old-time batteries. These things were huge, really big, like the first ones ever made. They were longer than I was.

"There were maybe a half dozen long, thick copper wires, thicker than a quarter inch, coming out of these things and were attached to insulator coils. It was all really strange.

"I know this sounds weird and remember this is a little kid's perception, but to me they looked like electrical parts used in Frankenstein's laboratory. I always wondered what all this was. My mother said Frank had used them. I think he was way ahead of his time.

"I wasn't supposed to, but I used to play in the ruins of the big house. I liked to dig there and was always finding silver coins. My mother thought Anna buried the money. If I brought any of the money into the house, my mother would build an extra hot fire using manzanita in the wood-burning stove and throw the coins in. She told me she did not want me handling or playing with any of that money again.

"One time while riding in the car, she caught me with some silver dollars. She took them from me and threw them out the window.

"When I started school, I used to buy bubblegum from other kids. I would give them a silver dollar for one piece of gum—they were always happy about that! Some kids used to give me a hard time. I didn't know why at the time but the more I hear about the Goat Doctor saga, I can see why."   **David**

David in front of goat barn   (Photo courtesy of David)

"I think something to do with spending money found on the land really spooked my Aunt Carmelita.

"When my uncle Lewey Dick was married to her, he told us she threw any silver coins they found into kitchen's wood burning stove and that there were always one or two big globs of silver among the ashes when he cleaned the stove out."   **M. Badeker**

Chapter Seven

After Carmelita sold the property in April of 1977, the new owner wanted to clear the land of brush and debris in preparation of building a home.

"Orval was asked by the current owner of the property to do some Cat (tractor) work. The old house had long-since burned and the only remaining part of the home was—you guessed it—the fireplace.

"Occasionally, Orval would wonder whatever happened to the money (in the hearth) and even mentioned it to his wife, but not to anyone else.

"As Orval was doing the work, he came upon the fireplace and was tempted to push it over with the cat. However, just in front of it stood a beautiful little cedar tree and you know how Orval feels about destroying live trees.

"Anyway, there was no way he could get to the fireplace without taking out the tree also. He wavered only a minute before moving away—leaving the tree and the fireplace still intact.

"After the forest fire in 1979, during a logging operation in preparation for a landing, a logger bulldozed over the fireplace and discovered the money. It was kept a secret for a while, but it is difficult in a small community to hide sudden wealth, so eventually it was made known that it had been found.

ORVAL BECKETT

"The finding of the treasure created all sorts of interest in that property, with the result that the owner asked Orval to see what he could find. Orval and Bill Smith searched and came up with several coins, but no great treasure."
L. Beckett-*Pearson*
L. Davies -
Mosquito Memories

"The new owner came over and again asked me to go over there and see what I could find; he told me I could keep half. He didn't live near there and people were tearing up the place real bad. He said he'd put a fence around the place but they'd just tear it down like the fences that had been there." **O. Beckett**

"People were always digging up the place. They were just plain ruthless." **V. Fancher**

"A well kept secret in town is that there was a third man along with the two loggers on the Goat Doctor's place when they dug up the money and hightailed it out of there that day, but he disappeared off the face of the earth." **Anonymous**

"One time I was in the Bank Café in Placerville. There were a couple of unsavory characters at a table next to us clinking silver dollars together. They sat there drinking and bragging about the money they had gotten by looting the place." **R. Weichold**

"It was common knowledge around these parts that just before it became known that a lot of money was found on Frank's place, there was a certain so-and-so who lived in the area who was seen over there digging up the place. People used to wonder how he was able to buy a new truck, a new television, and various other expensive items." **Anonymous**

The following is from the magazine **Treasure Found!**
Spring edition 1981
As told to Dave Weeks by Jimmy Sierra

"In November of 1979, a man we shall call Mr. Brown purchased 75 acres of land in the foothills, with the intention of building a home near the three old houses of the faith healer.

"Before he could do much more than build a foundation for his house, a forest fire ravaged much of the area, burning down most of the old buildings. (Called the Chili Bar Fire, it consumed 7,000 acres of timber and homes.)

"Discouraged, Brown decided to sell the property. He recruited a couple of lumberjacks who were working with the Forest Service camp nearby to come up with a Caterpillar grader to clear off the burned debris, including the old aluminum roofs which now lay on the ground.

"In the process, near what had been a tack house for animals, they cut into the corner of a large chest or trunk underground, spreading the contents over about a 150-foot long path. Suddenly, they realized they had spilled out coins—silver dollars and half dollars—and silver certificates in big rolls.

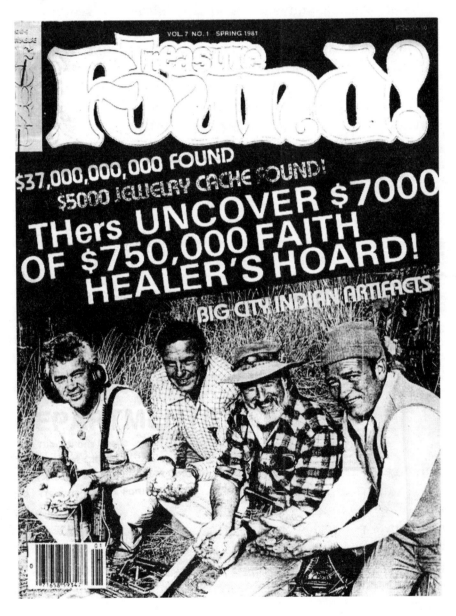

"So, they jumped off the Cat and stuffed their clothes with all this money and they wound up filling three five-gallon jerry cans, too. From what we could find out through second-hand information, there was a total of about five thousand silver dollars alone! The whole amount was certainly in excess of fifty thousand dollars market value.

"The lumberjacks packed up their treasure and left. They didn't show up at work any more, but apparently went straight downtown and started to spend these moldy $20 silver certificates and silver dollars in the bars, and got themselves politely pie-eyed for two days.

"Next, they turned up in South Tahoe, Nevada, at the casinos, doing the same thing, plopping the silver certificates and silver dollars right out on the blackjack tables. So, that's what happened to the bulk of the first cache.

"It wasn't long before the rest of the lumber camp got wind of what was going on and little by little men disappeared from their jobs and reappeared picking through the debris on the home site.

"As they were going over the area with shovels and picks, it suddenly dawned on one of the men that a metal detector would speed things up considerably, so he went down to Ray Bolduc, my dealer at Tahoe Treasure Cove (now in Placerville), and rented a detector.

"The fellow told how the second group of lumberjacks did well enough themselves: coins were so plentiful that they were sticking to the men's boots as they walked through the mud.

"This person never divulged the exact location, but Ray had lived in that area before, and from the sparse information he got, he figured out exactly where it was.

"Using the rented detector, and still eye-balling, the second group found perhaps two or three other caches, making a total of four in the vicinity of the main house.

"One had been hidden in the remains of the fireplace. The others were probably found around the perimeter of the house. The lumberjacks indicated that they found $1700 loose on the ground. Ray was pretty much convinced there would be even more caches besides the four that had been found already.

"Ray drove up to see for himself, and said the place looked a little like the remains of World War II, having been dug up by all kinds of people by now.

"'What shall we do about this treasure,' Ray asked me. I said, 'Let's get permission to go there. Sneaking in would be ill-advised, and we've got too much to lose to do that.'

"He agreed, and said the best way would be to get a contract with Mr. Brown, sign a search agreement, and split the find with him.

"But the owner rejected our written request saying, he was plagued by people who want to go in, meddle around and destroy his land. He wanted to kill the whole idea of the treasure. As far as he was concerned, everything had been found, and that was the end of that.

"For the most part of a year, we just sort-of sat tight. Then Ray thought he'd go up and see if the owner had restored order. Sure enough, there was a sheriff on patrol.

"But to Ray's surprise, it looked as if about a hundred more people had been digging, the land had changed that much. While he was in the hills, he stopped at a spring where everybody in the area stops, and had a drink of water.

"As he looked down, he spied a silver dollar in the rocks. Someone had probably stopped there to wash off his coins! We decided it was time to present our case again.

"That's when I called Ed Milota from Search and Recover in Ventura, California. Ed is a real professional who knows how to use a two-box detector, and who is also quite proficient with his 6000D.

"Coincidentally, Ed happened to have lived in the city where Mr. Brown was living, and thought he might know someone who knew the owner. Ed made contact with Brown, who was again negative, but because Ed was persistent, the man finally agreed to meet us in the foothills to talk about it.

"He had some other business there anyhow, which turned out to be a meeting with the people he was selling the property to.

"We met Brown at one in the afternoon, after much anxious moments in the morning. You can imagine how we felt when he announced: 'Well, I'm not so sure there's anything here. Lets forget the whole thing.'

"We had to spend the next fifteen minutes trying to convince him to just give us some time. We had traveled so far. Finally, he reluctantly consented. 'I'll give you till three o'clock.'

"Here we were, faced with 75 acres, and less than 120 minutes. We all took off in different directions. Ed took the two-box down below the old house. He immediately got a target, but it turned out to be the top of an old stove, about three and a half feet deep.

"Ray stopped at the old tack house, the first cache site, figuring if he got a single coin he could at least prove to the owner that there were still coins lying around. Sure enough he got a silver half about three seconds later.

"Meanwhile, Don took off to my left, and went right down the middle. Ray had commented while we were standing on a road overlooking the whole area that a particular large, isolated pine tree looked like a good hunting possibility.

"That was what we said to each other, but now I was headed in the other direction of that tree, working a few spots along an old goat path. I got a couple of wrong signals, aluminum here, other scrap metal there, and I walked around the tree.

"I was hunting in GEB Discriminate to counteract the heavily mineralized red mining dirt that covered the area. Working in straight TH wouldn't have given me the depth I wanted. Then I got a signal that sounded healthy...it was a silver dime, about four inches down.

"I thought, 'Well, That's it, that's all there is.' Actually, I was discouraged by the dime. Up until now, every coin from the site had been either a silver dollar or a silver half; to our knowledge, that's all the man had buried.

"Damn, someone just dropped a dime out of their pocket," I thought. Yet I made another pass, as I always do over a hole after I pull out a coin, and I was startled because this time a louder sound came out!

"Obviously, the target was very large, and when I put the 6000D into Normal mode, the signal was just too big. Still, my heart began to pump a little faster—I must admit it pounded a lot faster.

"I started to dig with my Buck knife, and about nine inches down I saw something I'll never forget: coins began to bubble out of the ground like seeds out of a broken pomegranate. All I could see were dimes and a few quarters, and I figured I had found a small cache. There really was something there!

"Getting the owner was my first reaction, because I

One group who went into the area said the silver dollars were just sticking to their feet!

"THE COINS BEGAN TO BUBBLE OUT LIKE THE SEEDS OF A BROKEN POMEGRANATE"

large garbage. We found that in

wanted him to be there when I dug it up. I had the feeling I was only going to find a handful of dimes, and quarters, and I didn't want him to think I had planted them just to show him a cache was there.

"Even if it was just a small handful, it would

be invaluable in getting us a contract. Or so I thought. I walked all the way back to the road to get him. 'I've got a small treasure to show you,' I said.

Jimmy Sierra poses with the cache, which weighed 40 pounds and completely filled the detector carrying bag.

"My voice was trembling, because I was still sort-of excited, but I didn't want to let on. I wanted to look every bit the professional to this man, like I do this all the time.

"When we got back to the hole, I started prodding and pushing and I couldn't believe my eyes as silver started coming out of the ground just like water, and then we started getting down to the big coins, and the hole was getting bigger and bigger.

"As it turns out, the coins, along with a toothbrush, two paper clips and a bottle opener, were all put together in a old bag, about the size of a small watermelon, which by now had disintegrated. The coins had consequently spread out underneath rocks and roots, so it took me about an hour and a half to extricate all the coins from the ground and to lay them out.

"The bottom of the old bag was maybe 18 or 20 inches underground, and really all that remained of it was a piece of material about as big as a handkerchief.

"Some of the coins were still in rotted old wrappers from the bank, and I spotted a roll of beautiful mint-condition quarters, which I didn't get the date of, but the dimes in a similar roll were 1935S, in absolutely mint condition.

"I didn't get a single one of those, and neither did any of the rest of us. We figure the whole roll went into a different pot.

"We noticed plenty of very valuable coins as we went along, although we didn't pay too much attention, because each handful produced so many more that it was truly mind boggling, and I was sort of numb.

"You asked me what the oldest coins were, and I think they would have to be a couple of 1878 Carson City dollars. I've got one here now.

"Others included an 1891S dollar in mint condition; an 1897S with an actual proof surface to it, which I also have here; and lots of Barber halves, Standing Liberty quarters and mercury dimes—in all, about 2200 coins, weighing about 40 pounds.

"Besides silver coins, some Indian Head pennies, Buffalo Head nickels and a few newer coins were near the top. There was also a Chinese silver coin, weighing 40-some-odd grams, bigger than a silver dollar. It was a Big Cash or Tael coin, from the old empire, I suppose.

"It had a dragon and all the writing around it, the first silver one I've ever seen. Altogether, our coins added up to $7000 in meltdown value!

"We still had fifteen minutes to go, and Brown said, 'I have to fly back at three o'clock, but before I sign any recovery contract, I think I'm going to have to see another cache.'

"We all just stopped stunned. We fell for it, even though now I think he was only half serious. Ray and I took off in a pair, helter-skelter, tripping over each other and getting caught in blackberry vines and poison oak, trying to find another signal in a hurry.

"Then I stopped and said, 'What are we doing? We're crazy. We're just running around in circles, he's got us like puppets on a string!'

"We went back to him and told him we weren't going to look any more that day, and that he either sign a contract now or forget it. 'I guess you're right, that's too much to ask,' he said.

"So, he signed the contract, which he has since cancelled, but we had it for the rest of the month. The property has now been sold. I assume he got a good price for it, and the man who bought it is probably going in there with a bulldozer, because rumor has it he thinks there are more caches to be found.

"When we left, we took a side road, because we didn't want to be seen with all this money. We drove down to the airport and laid the coins out on my wife's jacket.

"We made a big pile and cut it in half: half went to the owner of the land, and the other half we took down to the motel where we were staying, lined it up in four piles, and drew straws for each pile. We didn't check for dates or anything like that.

"You asked me if I felt strange at all at this place, and the answer is unmistakably, 'YES!' It's a very eerie feeling you get when you're standing at the side of that tack house.

"After Ray had pointed out the lone pine, I agreed it was a likely spot. But until I started walking toward it, the feeling hadn't sunk in. Then when I got near it, it was almost like I was compelled. I stopped two or three times to dig little targets, but honestly, I found I was not jumpy like I usually am, but very calm, almost serene.

"I started working as if I had all the time in the world, with nothing to stop me. I just walked right down the goat path, and it led me to that tree. Much later, I stopped to think, 'My goodness, what happened there?'

"I felt that I was totally calm, and that I had to do this thing. I was almost in a daze. The property owner mentioned later that it was meant to be, that it had to be done, even though he really wanted to stay away from the whole thing.

"Dowsing is all psychic power, I believe. I think that there are auras left behind. If this healer was really a strong psychic, then he had left energy behind in the ground, in the area. Something was left behind. But a lot of people won't buy that, unless it happens to them." *(end)*

"Chili Bar is just a few miles from old Doc André's place. During the Chili Bar fire of 1979, I was living in Lake Tahoe running a metal detector business. The fire was so bad the smoke had traveled clear to Lake Tahoe. Ashes even covered the cars.

"A man and his wife came into my shop to rent a metal detector but didn't know how to use it. After I instructed them on the use of one, we kept on visiting.

"He said he was a Caterpillar driver with a logging crew. He told how two of the men on the crew had unearthed a large stash of money, mainly silver dollars, while hired to clear off some land for a man whose property wasn't far from Chili Bar.

"This man and his wife wanted to try their luck at finding some coins. I had lived near the area he was talking about for six months in 1969. From what he said, I was pretty sure I knew the area he was talking about.

"I couldn't get away immediately, but finally, three or four weeks later, I took off down the mountain.

"My wife and I had heard tales about the Goat Doctor burying money all over the place on his property. After his cabin burned down, we were hearing what seemed like everybody and his uncle digging for gold and silver on old Doc André's land.

"So my wife and I decided we would give it a try. We liked the Goat Doctor but he was dead and gone. We had heard the widow just threw the coins she found into the fireplace, so why not try!

"We went over there in the middle of the night with lights on our caps like miners wore and dug for awhile. There was still a lot of tarpaper and other debris all around the foundation; burnt household items, lots of melted door latches, nails, etc.

"We went behind the foundation a ways, near the creek. I had brought a metal detector and we had just gotten a reading when we saw the lights of a car coming towards the property.

"We decided to high-tail it out of there. Every time we tried to go back on the property, someone was there.

"Later, after the owner gave permission to search the land, I found quite a few coins – I gave them all to the Placerville Museum. They have it on display there to this day. We heard shortly after that the owner had given the land to Jimmy Swaggart.

"In 1981, a sister or sister-in-law to Carmelita came into my metal detector shop in Lake Tahoe. We talked about the Chili Bar fire of '79. She told me how Carmelita was in tears over the fire.

"I heard that during a probate sale of Doc André's estate, someone bought the Goat Doctor's truck. Under the frame of the truck, a conduit had been welded and capped at both ends. The conduit was filled with silver coins—$40,000.00 worth!"**R. Bolduc**

"I think the story about money in a pipe under their truck was just Hollywood hype."

G. Milham- Desjardin

Excerpts from **Discover Magazine**
'Faith Healer's Hoard And The Hand Of Faith',
1st quarter, 1981, White's Electronics – by Ed Hart.

"The lumberjacks took more than fifty thousand dollars from the cache and over the next few weeks other treasure hunters dug up another seventeen hundred dollars worth.

"Could it be the tip of a larger iceberg? Needless to say, when the owner of the land heard of the discovery, he shut down the property and refused to allow any further digs. As it turns out, it took more than a year of selling to budge the fellow, and who can blame him?

"So here was Jimmy Sierra grinding along the back roads of the Mother Lode to take a shot at what may have been an empty trove. Another hunter, Ed Milota of Search and Recover in Ventura, helped convince the owner that it would be worth another search.

"Still, all Jimmy and Ed could talk the fellow into were two hours. Wow, 2 hours to search eighty-five acres! Jimmy had asked Don Arthur, president of the South Lake Tahoe Treasure Hunting club to help out.

"Jimmy's heart was pounding as they reached the general area of the old man's cabin. The foundation sits on a slanted table of land above a ravine in which a slow running brook ran. It was surrounded by towering firs and pine trees.

"The smell of the Sierra this time of year was almost enough to inspire a painter to paint, a poet to write. God! How he loves this country.

"As they moved down the canyon, one of the men remarked that a tall pine at the edge of the clearing looked like a good place for a cache. The three were so excited that they barely tuned their metal detectors before the search was on.

"Ray headed for the ruins of the foundation while Jimmy began to check around some nearby trees. The soil in this part of the Mother Lode is highly charged with minerals and it takes a real pro and much patience to fine-tune an instrument. Even the legendary COINMASTER 6000/D needed careful balancing.

"Jimmy finally moved around to the right of the big pine tree. 'Whump!' It was a good, strong discriminate signal. Jimmy stooped down and uncovered a silver dime.

"His heart began to pound even faster and his instrument sounded an even louder alarm. Jimmy was on all fours now, scratching the dirt, beneath the big tree. He knew he had the glory hole, and soon the coins began to bubble from the ground.

"Silver dimes, quarters, halves, Barbers, Mercurys, Walking, and Standing Liberties. Then came the Silver Dollars. The coins had been buried in a large bank bag that had rotted with time and the coins had settled in the red dirt and rock within the roots of the tree.

"Jimmy was more than two hours just cleaning out this one hole and he was sure there was more. Twenty-two hundred coins in all, the silver value alone was more than seven thousand dollars.

"For Jimmy, this was the 'BIG' one. The happy owner took fifty percent of the find and the hunters divided the rest. But, again, it was not the money, it was the find. They would negotiate for further digs, but this trip home from the Mother Lode would be one Jimmy Sierra was to savor for months to come." *(end)*

"There were so many varying accounts and amounts told about the loggers who stole the money, that I think only the men themselves really know the facts. The most often told and I think most people believed is they got close to $60,000. After their arrest, they purportedly returned half to the owner, who then agreed not prosecute."

G. Milham- Desjardin

218

The following excerpts are from **Treasure Found!**
Summer, 1981:

"After our story hit the newsstands, Jimmy Sierra was
approached by one of the men who found the $50,000—a

lumberjack—who said the story was accurate, except for one minor detail.

"The two lumberjacks were not the first ones to find treasure on the site, as we all had surmised, for they too had been told long before setting foot on the property (to clear an area for construction purposes, at the behest of the new owner), that there were more caches waiting to be found.

"In fact, two other men had first stumbled across an underground vault on the land. This makeshift bank was a four-foot-by-four-foot wooden structure, holding twenty thousand dollars face value in gold coin!

"The lumberjack further told Jimmy that these original treasure finders were now living in Nevada, retired millionaires, supposedly from the sale of the gold coins when bullion value hit nearly seven hundred dollars an ounce.

"As a final tantalizing jab, the teller of this story said that the finders of the gold coins would eventually come out with the full story for FOUND, but that obviously they would like to wait a few more years before doing so.

"You may dismiss this all as a creation of someone's fertile imagination, as the story is a third-hand account. But for those of us here who saw the silver recovered from that site, and who have read time and again actual contemporary biographies of the faith healer containing facts which we were asked to withhold from the story, you would undoubtedly feel as we do that it was not only possible a large gold coin cache was found, but almost a certainty." *(end)*

"One stash reportedly discovered on the property was a quarter of a million dollars worth of gold and jewelry." **J. (Sierra) Normandi**

'Goat Doctor's' treasure found; more lies waiting?

Mountain Democrat
December 4, 1981 - by Pat Lakey

Excerpt:
"For decades people from around the world flocked to the Mosquito district north of Placerville seeking the "Goat Doctor's" mystic healings. Now they come seeking his money.

"For the past two years, tales have abounded of buried treasures amounting to hundreds of thousands of dollars having been unearthed on the late Francis Andre's property eight miles from Placerville. Andre, more popularly known as the Goat Doctor because of a large herd of goats that roamed his land, is said to have buried much of his reportedly vast fortune before his death in 1959.

"Now, more than 20 years later, silver coins and other treasures are being discovered on the 85-odd acres, although the two Placerville developers who bought the property six months ago would rather not mention it.

"The story unfolded about a month ago when the Mountain Democrat received an anonymous telephone call from a man who said he had seen several people on the property with metal detectors and bulldozers and that they were uncovering great quantities of money.

"When a reporter arrived there less than an hour later, however, the property was deserted, although the land appeared ravaged by bulldozer blades.

"During the next few days, hints of the Goat Doctor's treasure kept surfacing, but remained vague as far as pinpointing exactly what was now being found on the André's former homestead.

"A tip from Paul Bailey, owner of Sports Unlimited in Placerville, rekindled the story about two weeks ago. Bailey said he sold a metal detector to a man 'who knew exactly what (brand) he wanted and paid cash for it.' Bailey said it wasn't long before he 'put two and two together'.

"Bailey told the Democrat he knew for a fact that thousands of dollars worth of silver coins had been found on the property because he is acquainted with one of the professional treasure hunters who was hired to search the land in October 1980.

"Bailey produced magazines published by the metal detecting firms that told of the treasure hunters' find, said to amount to several thousand dollars in silver coins uncovered within two hours. The owner at that time, Brian Dir, apparently then told the hunters not to search further.

"But the stories left blank what has happened on the land since the discoveries, made more than a year ago.

"Six months ago, two developers purchased the property with the intention of subdividing the land and selling parcels, according to Lee Wilson of Century 21 realty in Placerville. The Pair of owners are Wilson's clients.

"Wilson told the Democrat that coins currently are being found 'hither and yon' on the property, although he said two teams of professional treasure hunters hired by the owners to search the area "didn't find much."

"'It's been a real headache for me, because we've had a lot of trouble with people coming in here at night with metal detectors trying to find something,' Wilson said, 'We keep an eye on the place, but it has been a lot of trouble'.

"Wilson said the owners purchased the André's former property because it was a 'sound investment' and not because there was a possibility of having treasure there. He concedes, however, that every time the land has been searched at the direction of the owners, 'something has been found'.

"The question is, of course, how much remains to be uncovered? Some residents of the Mosquito district believe the old Goat Doctor may have buried as much as $750,000.

"'That's a bucket of malarky,' said Orval Beckett, who has lived in the area since 1933 and was a friend of the Goat Doctor. Beckett, 69, said the doctor used to ask Beckett to take the doctor's money to the bank in Placerville whenever Beckett made the trip along the winding road—in those days not paved—that crosses the American River Canyon about a mile south of the André's former property. Beckett lives about a mile from the doctor's old home.

"'I know for a fact that most of his money went into the bank,' Beckett told the Democrat. 'There was a time once when Dr. André told me he wanted to show me something and he took me to look at his fireplace. There was a loose stone in the hearth and inside there was an earthen jar and some other containers filled with coins'.

"'Dr. André told me he wanted me to know where it was so that in the event of his death I could tell his mom and dad about the money. But it couldn't have been more than 10 or 15 thousand dollars'.

"'The fireplace stash apparently was unearthed in 1979 by firemen and loggers fighting the Chili Bar fire,' Beckett said. Wilson confirmed that story.

"'Two years ago the cat-skinners and loggers found coins rolling out of the flue, and they took off with the money,' Wilson said."

"After selling the property, we moved to my mother's [Carmelita] home-town for a while and then to Madison, California where we ended up living next to a migrant camp.

"When I was 14 years old, we were living in Woodland, California. We were dirt poor, living in poverty, and basically starving to death. My mother had given away everything except some boxes of Frank's medical journals.

"One day, I went into the Nugget Market. I liked to read a lot. In the market, I picked up a magazine called *Treasure*. On the front of the magazine, in big letters, was "The Goat Doctor's Hoard Found."

"I could have had a heart attack. I didn't have enough money to buy the magazine so I went home to try to find some. I dug through the chairs and sofa for loose change but there was no money there. I ran around collecting Seven-Up bottles to get the refunds on them until I had enough to buy the magazine.

"I was always miffed about the treasure. I saw what poverty had done to my mom."   **David A.**

Five pictures—taken in 1997, when the then owner of the Goat Doctor property held his annual treasure hunt day. He invited people to come for the day, bring their metal detectors and search for coins.

Above shows treasure hunters nearing where the cabin once stood. This was the view from inside the André's' cabin, although the trees and bushes are less dense now due to the forest fire of 1979 and tractors have leveled off the rugged, hilly land and deep drive.

The pickings are getting slimmer, however, the hunters were not disappointed. The last hunt yielded 47 coins, and considering they date back fifty to ninety years, some are quite valuable.

"I grew up on that property and I know a place on the other side of a certain mountain that I'd bet anything—there's money buried there." **David A.**

"Look here sweetheart, there's no money buried on that land, I know! Those people were as poor as paupers and if you ever saw the place, you'd know. He didn't even charge people for treating them, and what people did leave him as a donation, he gave that all away too."   **L. Wagner**

"Frank told me, 'Someday these grounds are going to be dug up and a lot of people are going to be surprised.'"   **I. Meadows**

"I thought Frank didn't have enough money for shoes. No one, but no one, could have been more shocked than I was when I first heard of all the silver, gold and paper money buried on Frank's land."
Don Thompsen

"When I first heard about all that money buried on the property, all I could think of, for days, was how my husband, Frank's accountant, would have discounted all the stories—he'd never have believed them."   **E. Kamp**

"The Goat Doctor's real treasure was in his powers of healing and you cannot imagine the hundreds, upon hundreds, of people that man healed."
O. Beckett

In 1985, James (Sierra) Normandi—White's Electronics, Inc. of California in San Rafael and White's Electronics, Inc. in Sweet Home, Oregon (Corporate manager- Alan Holcombe) funded a film entitled "Quest for Treasure". Made for television by Creekside Productions and hosted by actor Clint Walker.

The following letter was written to the owners of the Goat Doctor property in 1986:

"It has come to our attention, that you are intending to sell some 69 acres in Mosquito, California. We are residents of Mosquito, which is about nine miles north of Placerville and we wonder if we could have a moment of your time to express our feelings concerning the future of this land.

"We have no business interest in this land. We simply would like to have it set aside and preserved as it is. Maybe we can clarify to you our feelings about this historical site.

"At least three of us, and many more, actually, have had to them communicated a sense of urgency concerning the preservation of this land.

"In 1911, the approximately 300 acres were owned by the André family, Ernest and Anna, and their adopted son Frank. Their presence in our little valley is etched for all time.

"In the hearts of those who received their limitless love, for they gave their love to all those around them, and even though they have passed on, their love still endures as the young people of the community listen to their stories and carry them in their hearts and pass them down to their young.

"Ernest was a poet, his verses as timeless as the land itself as he drew strength from the energy in these hills. His wife, Anna, was psychic, and when you hear the old-timers mention this as matter-of-factly as the weather, you know they had good reason to forget their skepticism.

"It was she that saw her young son, Frank, as a healer of the sick and injured and so provided the catalyst for what was to become the famous Goat Doctor, Mr. Frank André. He was a quiet soul that amazed patients as well as physicians with his special ability to comfort and cure many that all else had given up on.

"Money was not his motivation—love and understanding of a higher power were the driving power behind his desire to accommodate those that sought his touch. He never considered himself successful, merely a willing instrument, through which love and energy could be funneled.

"On reading the accounts of the Andrés, it may occur to one that this land is rich in history—and so it is. But it is much more than that. Devastating fires have swept through the area more than once, but this does not begin to take away from the sacredness of the place.

"I use the word sacred because no other seems to describe the feelings experienced by those of us who have journeyed to the top of the hill to the family gravesite.

"There is an energy of life and love here, that cannot, adequately, be described with words.

"It is timeless, and if you can imagine a huge open-aired church with the river rushing below, the wind whispering through the pines and the eagles soaring effortlessly down the canyon, you would begin to feel our love and protectiveness towards this place.

"Please do not pass these lines off as idle romanticism, for we are all hard working people with many other obligations. It is just that we feel that this land must survive as it is.

"People must be allowed to come and visit this strange and drawing place, as we have, and if they are able, to take with them a part of the love and energy that generates here. It is said that a powerful healer can put energy into his surroundings that will survive long after his spirit is freed. Whatever the source, it is here and we are asking you to please help preserve it.

"If we had the money to buy the land and set it aside for all those who need to visit it, we would. But we do not. Perhaps there is another way. It would be possible to set up a non-profit organization within the Community of Mosquito supported by responsible citizens who could be caretakers of the land.

"We believe there would be high public support of this, as the Goat Doctor was known throughout Northern California and abroad due to his love for his fellow beings and for all of the misery he has alleviated.

"Such a donation would never be forgotten in this spiritually minded country. We hope this letter has reached you in a generous and understanding time and that you have had the patience to bear with us while we try to restrain our emotions and present our plea the best way we know how.

"May we hear from you on this? And please, you are more than welcome to visit our little community anytime you wish at Finnon Lake Resort, which is the heart of this Mosquito District.

"We know that if you were to visit the hilltop meadow, you, too, would sense something there and this place would never be forgotten to you.

"Thank you for your kind attention."

Gwen Reid   Owner, Finnon Lake
Clarissa Darr   Mosquito Resident
Steve Laymon   Mosquito Resident

They received no response to the letter.

———————

"The Hunt for Amazing Treasures"

The story of "The Goat Doctor Treasure," also known as "The Faith Healers Hoard," was related in "The Hunt for Amazing Treasures", a NBC special which aired on national television in March of 1995 and then repeated in September of 1995. This program and segments of it were sold to Discovery Channel and were aired many times during the following years. It aired four times on Christmas day 1999.

Sandra Farrell Bazrod published a book in 1999, based on the television series "The Hunt For Amazing Treasures" that included Jimmy Sierra's story about "The Faith Healers Hoard".

Additional patient stories:

"Bill's sister was four years old when she was caught by the hay pulley cable and was pulled upward and then dropped off to the ground.

"As she grew, she began to be in so much pain and unable to do even simple chores.

"The doctors told her parents that she would steadily get worse, and would be in a wheelchair and unable to have children. In the early twenties, someone told the parents about the Goat Doctor.

"They were living in Elk Grove at the time and she was about nine years old. They went to him and he treated her several times. She was never a cripple. She grew, married, and had two children.

"Cars were there all night, lined up, even people from Europe."   **M. Waggersman**

"He used to advocate, 'If you want to stay healthy, keep away from white sugar, white flour and drink goats milk.' He said raw sugar was okay."

L. Wagner

"When my Uncle Bud was seventeen years old, he was working in the tunnel of a chromium mine, out of Folsom.

"He was in the blacksmith shop, cleaning out his carbide lamp when a large door, propped up with a stick, was knocked down by someone coming through the door.

"He was hit on the head with the iron-door latch, and then knocked backwards over the anvil. He landed in the 'slag tub' full of water which was used to put the hot iron in to temper it.

"He was unconscious and wondered many times why he never drowned. The miners from the tunnel found him much later.

"The one who knocked the door down didn't realize that Bud had been hurt at all. Bud was taken to the hospital in Folsom then transferred to a hospital in Sacramento where he laid unconscious for four days.

"While in Sacramento they put him in traction, which had no positive results for his injured back.

"He worked from then on in a local garage in Diamond Springs. Always in chronic pain, he would get so stove-up he could hardly bend. Finally, in 1925 he learned of Frank André and began going to him.

"The doctor's adjustments were gentle but strong enough to begin to break down the misalignment and he had relief for the first time."   **R. Gust**

"I worked for the State of California auto repair shop. One of the fellows in the shop had his back go out and couldn't stand up straight.

"He had heard the other men at the shop talk about going to the Goat Doctor for various ailments. When all else failed after being seen by a few expensive doctors in Sacramento, he was taken to the Goat Doctor, who fixed him up in ten minutes.

"When I found I had somehow put my back out-of-whack, I went to the Goat Doctor. He was still called Frank then, not doctor.

"The dirt road from Placerville to Mosquito was so thick with dust you couldn't see the holes and bumps. It was rough!

"Once while I was there, a woman was brought to him that had been in such a bad accident that the car ended up looking like an accordion.

"There was no way anyone could forget it. She was in an absolutely, horrible condition. The accident had left the poor soul with her legs locked, crossed and up over her shoulders.

"I was told the pitiful looking woman had been in the hospital for several weeks and had every kind of specialist come to Placerville to try to treat her.

"It took Frank André six treatments to correct the woman's predicament, but she did walk again on her own because of him." **C. Bovey**

"I first heard of the Goat Doctor in 1928. My husband told me of seeing him on his foothill ranch, winter and summer, barefoot and in jeans. This was when he was trying to heal himself of tuberculosis.

"He helped me many times. I often put my lower back out. Sometimes the pain was excruciating and he always cured it with one treatment." **D. Radon**

"My recollection of the Goat Doctor goes back to the early 1930's. My father awakened me at dawn. He was in excruciating pain and his stomach was all swelled up like a poisoned pup.

"He had overdone on red wine and bananas at a party the night before.

"He said he wanted to go see André, the Goat Doctor. Being a smart teenager and a loving son, I suggested a regular MD. He said that they would cut him open, but André could fix him up without surgery.

"We lived in the town of El Dorado. I drove through Placerville and out the steep, narrow Mosquito Road to the Andrés.

"Dad was in great pain and alternated between 'Hurry up—I'm hurting,' and 'Slow down—are you trying to kill us?'

"Arriving at André's, I parked on the edge of the road and my father climbed through the fence and went into the house. I waited anxiously in the car.

"In less than an hour Dad came out feeling great and his waistline was down to it's normal 44 inches.

"Move over." he said, I'm driving home."

"He had nothing but praise for André. It seemed like everyone held André in high esteem." **H. Hoover**

"The first time I actually went to him was in the 30's when I went with a disabled friend of mine. He came clear from Los Angeles to see him.

"He got instant relief, so when my back was injured I went to him for treatment. He was good and I continued going to him 'til I left there in 1931. At that time, it was $1 or nothing a treatment, whatever a person could spare." **F. Fausell**

"I was young, married, and living in San Francisco. I had a slipped vertebra that was always going out. I was bent over with pain. After having no luck with doctors in my area — I heard about the Goat Doctor. It was a very long trip, to get to his place, but very worth it because he always helped me." **D. Narkus**

"My mother had cataracts and couldn't see very well. Everything was shiny to her.

"Anyway, she liked to paint things. She painted the old Model-T and we swore she painted it with a broom. One day while painting the house, she slipped, the window was open, and she hit the sill.

"Her whole arm turned blue. She didn't go to the doctor. She used to pull the bucket from the well and she couldn't do that anymore she hurt so much. She couldn't even comb her hair. Then she began having awful pain when she'd get up. You could see she was hurting.

"My sister asked her if she'd like to have the Goat Doctor take a look at her shoulder.' My mom said, 'Okay'. We went and he worked on her shoulder and straightened it out in one treatment.

"Another time, this fellow I know called me and asked if I could tell him how to get to the Goat Doctors.

"It was stormy weather and I couldn't work. I told him it was hard to find, and that if he wanted, I'd go with him.

"So we took the trip all the way up there, with him moaning and hurting all the way. We got him in and put him on the table.

"Pretty soon the Goat Doctor said to him, 'You know you had a very bad accident at one time.' The fellow said he had got bucked off a horse sometime back.

"The Goat Doctor said, 'Well I'll tell you what I've got to do. I've got to tear this all loose and this is going to hurt a little bit.'

"It was already hurting him! Anyway, the doctor gave him his treatment and told him to come back there another time. So, then we left.

"The next day, the fellow's son called me and said his dad was in such pain he had to take him to the hospital the night before. I thought, what the heck, why did we take him up there for in the first place!

"Well, the Goat Doctor must have loosened something because what ever it was, the fellow passed it while in the hospital and never had any more trouble! From then on, every time I saw this fellow he'd ask, 'Have you seen the Goat Doctor?' He thought so highly of him."

H. Rominger

"My wife's Uncle Milt was District Ranger for the Forest Service. I went to see him one day. Milt was hobbling around, still! He'd been that way the last time I had seen him. He had a heck of a time walking.

"The doctor he'd been to had prescribed specially built shoes because he had fallen arches, but the shoes didn't make any difference. He was still hobbling around and growling.

"I asked, 'What's wrong with you Milt?'

"'I've got fallen arches,' he growled.

"I said, 'Oh hell Milt. It's not your arches—it's your hips! All you've gotta do is go out and see the Goat Doctor.'

"Milt growled back, 'You damned old fool. Maybe you think you know what's wrong with me but you don't!'

"Finally, as a last resort, Milt went to the Goat Doctor. After two or three treatments, he was fine. His arches were all right. It was his back!

"Ever since I could remember, my own mother had what doctors called sciatic rheumatism. So often, I saw that poor soul lying in bed crying. She was in such agony! I couldn't count the number of times my father and I would turn her on a sheet. It was pathetic. My mother's knees were so swollen and she had pain throughout her body. She couldn't get her arms up to comb her hair!

"For a year and a half, my 15-year old sister had to do it for her. I said to her one day, 'Mama, I'd be happy to take you down to see Frank.' She didn't answer me.

"Every day, I'd tell her the same thing until one day she said, 'Oh Orval, you're a nut on that Goat Doctor!' So—I just stopped saying it.

"Then one day she said, 'Orval, I'll go see the Goat Doctor if you'll take me.' By golly, I hustled around and got us ready to see him. Frank put her on his treatment table and did an adjustment on her spine for just a few minutes.

"We got about half way home and my wife, Lois, asked Mama, 'Are you feeling okay?' She said, 'That doctor may think he knows what he's doing, but he didn't even look at my knees!'

"The next morning after that treatment, she was sitting there combing her hair. I asked, 'How do you feel Mama?'

"She said, 'Orval, I'm combing my hair!' Then she pulled her skirt up to show her knees and said, 'Look at that! The swelling and the pain are all gone.'

"She was shocked! She had lived with it for so long! Now she could get up and move about.

"I said, 'Well Mama, maybe the Goat Doctor knew what he was doing after all.' Mama decided from then on out he was all right.

"I remember there was this lady from Sutter Creek who came over. She was a large lady who hadn't walked in three years!

"She had accidentally stepped backwards off a porch with a clothesbasket full of wet laundry she'd set out to hang.

"She'd been bedfast since that time, leaving the bed only to go to some hospital or doctor for treatments. They hadn't been able to do anything for her and had sent her home to wait for a set date for surgery, which she was dreading.

"So, in desperation, as she herself told the Goat Doctor, 'I came to see you!'

"As she lay on the treatment table, he worked on her for about 20 minutes. Then, he set her up on the side of the table and asked her how she felt.

236

"'Somewhat better,' she answered.

"He then told her, 'Stand up.'

"'Doctor, I can't,' she said.

"'I think you can,' he replied, 'You just try.' He had big, powerful hands that were as soft as baby skin.

"He helped her to stand, then he stepped back a few feet and said, 'Now walk over to me.'

"Again, she said, 'Doctor, I can't.'

"'You don't know unless you try,' he urged.

"She took one step and another. He stepped back a few more feet and stopped. She walked to him then practically fell into his arms.

"She wasn't off balance, she was just so grateful! She threw her arms around him and cried a bucket of tears!

"He had her lay down again and gently massaged her back. Then he put hot water bottles on her back and had her rest for a while. Within another 10 minutes, the lady walked out, still crying.

"As she left, the doctor told her he wanted to see her again in three or four days if she felt like it. I was cutting wood for the doctor the day she returned and watched her get out of the car, just like she'd never had a problem."   **O. Beckett**

"Rudy and I were up on Hotchkiss Hill cutting wood. We cut wood for the miners in Georgetown for $1.50 a cord.

"I bent over to pick up a block of wood, my back locked out of place and I couldn't move. Rudy drove me over to the Goat Doctor.

"It took well over an hour to drive down the hill and then up to Mosquito. When we got there, I couldn't move and had to be carried in.

"The Goat Doctor was a gentle person and was very concerned about my condition when he took me in to lie down.

"He used hot water bottles on my back, then I would rest for a while and he would return and massage my back to get things straightened out.

"Two or three vertebrae in my back had locked out. He would see other patients while I rested.

"I can testify that old boy knew what he was doing. I was carried in there because I couldn't walk, and three hours later I walked out!"   **G. Fogal**
                     P. Presba - Georgetown Gazette

"My brother, who was a highway foreman in Placerville, insisted I go see the goat Doctor. Three doctors had failed to help me so I expected the same results at this place.

"I was thirty-two years old at the time, having had back trouble since about age fifteen I had learned to live with it.

"It was around 10 a.m., I would guess. A knock on the door brought a medium-sized man with a small chin beard, hair in a bunch at the back of his neck, to greet us. We're invited in and asked what our trouble is. I explained my back trouble.

"The floor is covered with goat hides. The table he asks me to lie on is covered with goat hides.

"After a quick check of my hips and legs, he steps back and says to me, 'I can make a well man of you.'

"After a few more manipulations, I had no pain. I asked when he wanted to see me again, 'Only if it troubles you.' He never wanted you to return unless you hurt.

"When I asked his charge, he said, "Whatever you can pay." I always paid the going charge at other doctor's; it was two or three dollars. One dollar was the amount left by most people at this time.

"The Goat Doctor was great and the only one who could fix my back. I sent several patients to him, all were happy." **J. McFadden**

"I met Frank André in the thirties. I was born in nearby Pilot Hill. Every year on the third or fourth-of July, I used to make a cattle drive from Pilot Hill to Georgetown over many miles of rugged terrain.

"We would cross the Rubicon River, way up onto Brushy Springs, where we rented some land from the Forest Service.

"One very rough year, seven steers disappeared. In searching for them, my horse stumbled and I fell and injured my back.

"I was taken to one doctor after another. Finally, I went to the Goat Doctor. He fixed me up just fine after just one treatment.

"I would have felt even better if the sheriff had caught the villains who stole our cattle."

"I remember the doctor recommending bear clover and mountain misery for teas. It got the name mountain misery from the cowboys. Because, when they rode horse through very much of it, they'd end up with a headache.

"Anna used to come in the room where Frank was working and pray for people while he worked on them." **G. Gardner**-author of Georgetown Divide

"While working at the lime plant in Diamond Springs about 1938 or 1939, I injured my back.

"I went to two local doctors and to two chiropractors. The medical doctors wanted to operate, but from what I heard, about two thirds of the people who had surgery were no better off than the third not operated on.

"I was in chronic pain. I heard of the Goat Doctor so decided I'd go see him.

"At 7 o'clock in the morning, ours was about the seventh car back. Once inside, he put me in a small room near the treatment room.

"He had two or three goatskins instead of a mattress piled one on top of the other on top of a wood table. He worked on me on seven or eight different occasions.

"He said he wasn't a chiropractor. He was very thorough in what he did. He told me I had a partially herniated disc. Dr. André said, 'I can get the disc back in place, but there's one spot that's weak.'

"The last time I saw him, he kept me there all day. He worked on one patient, then on me, then on another patient, then back to me. This continued all day.

"Finally, with tears in his eyes, he came back to me and told me he couldn't help me. He told me I could have a special belt made, but in wearing it, it would weaken the muscles. He said, 'If you can stand the pain, you'd be better off in the long run.'

"There was a plate on a little table by the door if someone wanted to leave money, but he never charged me a cent. He was gentle, kind, and honest. He was unique."   **R. Haley**

"I had a bad chest cold and was real congested. I asked Frank what he thought I should do about it. He said he'd take care of it. He spread a thick coat of some kind of goop all over my chest.

"Next thing I knew, I was no longer congested, and my cold was gone. However, the poultice had set up as hard as the shell on a turtle, and I couldn't get it off. My chest hair stuck to it and began pulling to where it hurt.

"Then it caused a rash and I itched like crazy. My wife and I tried everything we could think of to get it off, with no luck. Finally, I asked my father-in-law to rip the darn thing off. He gave it one good tug, and I guess he could hear the pain in the yelp I let out, 'cuz he stopped right there.

"He said, 'Orval, you've always been a good son-in-law, you've never done anything to hurt me, and I just can't do this.' Finally, my wife managed to cut the hair little by little and we broke the blasted thing off."

O. Beckett

"It seemed like half the folks in Auburn and Newcastle went to him. I knew one fellow who was dang near blind. The Goat Doctor gave him some kind of a liquid solution made out of herbs and had him rinse his eyes out with it and danged if he didn't get his eyesight back."

G.Voyiatzes

"A friend of my mother's, a well-known society lady in Placerville, was in a bad car accident. She was treated by a few doctors who said there was nothing more they could do for her.

"For nine months, she was bedridden. My mother talked my father and a friend into putting her in our car and taking her over to see Frank. He worked on her three times during the one day. When he was done, she was able to walk up the hill to the car.

"Everybody around here that we knew had a story like this they could tell you.

"I'm pretty sure it was Mother André who said that she and Ernest also had TB at one time. She told me she, Ernest, and Frank used to sleep on beds of pine needles.

"My husband was told to report to the recruiting station. I had to drive him there. He was flat on his back and could barely walk. They put him through these tests they had to do. They listed him as crippled and said they couldn't use him. He was 4-F.

"We took him to the Goat Doctor right after that, he treated him two or three times, and he was fine and back to work."   **C. Neilsen**

"I was a pallbearer and had lifted the casket in such a way that my back went out and I was very bad off. I began going to Dr. André and he got me back on my feet.

"When I was in charge of the Placerville Lumber Company at Fresh Pond, I took many employees out to Dr. André when they would get hurt on the job and they'd be back at work the very next day."   **H. West**

"I had to seek help from Frank when I was working for Michigan-Cal Lumber in Pino Grande. There was a long cable called a bull-chain that was powered by a winch.

"It would drop down into the pond and we'd hook it onto the green Sugar Pine logs to pull them into the mill. One time, the hook came loose, swung around, hitting me in the chest.

"It knocked me over and somehow dislocated my neck in the fall. Some of the men took me to Frank. He had me stay in his cabin for three days.

"He treated me slowly with massages to my neck and got me back on my feet. I feel he saved my life. All the men at Michigan Cal called him 'God's gift to the human race.'

"Many times, we took people to him. Some were in quite bad shape. He healed damn near every one of them. He would tell people if he couldn't help them.

"One time a woman was there with a stomach problem. He sent her to her doctor. Another time, a man had a large lump on his neck and he told that man to go to a medical doctor."   **A. Boeding**

"I used to work at a gas station in Placerville. This was when there was no freeway. Placerville was the main thoroughfare for anyone coming from San Francisco or anywhere up north.

"During the course of three years, I cannot begin to tell you how many times I was asked, 'How do you get to Dr. André's', or 'How do I get to the Goat Doctor's?'

"I'd always tell them to really pay attention to my directions as he lived way out in the boon-docks and they would easily get lost or miss his place.

"Many of the cars had someone lying on makeshift beds. I talked with people from Arizona, Chicago and all over the United States."   **W. Weichold**

"I remember the Goat Doctor walking into the room. He was barefoot, wrinkled and had long, long hair. He seemed very old to me. I had not been around anyone that old and especially NO ONE with that long of hair!

"I was afraid of him when I first saw him and in awe of him at the same time. I remember how very nice and gentle he talked."   **D. Montgomery**

"After I had been diagnosed with stomach ulcers, given pills and told that if they didn't help I'd have to have surgery, I went out and talked with Dr. André. He told me to get some fresh cabbage, put it in a blender, and drink the juice. I healed almost immediately and never had a stomach problem from then on."   **L. Archer**

"In 1943, in Pilot Hill, California, a man rode into our yard and asked if anyone wanted to ride his horse. Dummy here said, 'I do.' Something spooked the horse and he threw me off. My right foot got caught in the stirrup and he dragged me for several hundred feet.

"How I got out of that stirrup, I don't know. I was out cold. When I came to, EVERYONE in Pilot Hill was in our house, even the owners of the local store, Mr. & Mrs. Dick Nance.

"I was a bloody pulp and had a great deal of pain in my badly injured right knee. The owner of the horse said he would pay for the Goat Doctor to work on my knee.

"It took months before my knee would hold me up. Dr. André had received a true gift from God to heal people. There were Angora goatskins everywhere and live Angora goats in the yard."   **J. Loomis**

"My mother, stepfather, and I went out there on many occasions. My mother had been a contortionist in a vaudeville act from age three.

"It was a family act and they traveled all over the country. My mother ended up with curvature of the spine and was in excruciating pain. As she got older, the condition worsened.

"More than once we had to wait for hours even though we usually got there at six in the morning. There would be at least a dozen cars ahead of us. I remember seeing many different out of state license plates.

"There was always a big pile of wood there. I would get so bored I would chop wood for an hour or so, then, someone else would usually take over right after me.

244

"She had been to chiropractors in Oregon, Arizona, Nevada, Washington and California. The Goat Doctor was the only one who was able to help her. This shows his capability and knowledge in treating people."   **D. Dodge**

"My son was six at the time. We'd buy him a new pair of shoes, the best shoes we would find, but in two weeks, they'd be run over so badly that the heels were pretty well vertical with the flat of his soles.

"Our doctor said we should get to Sacramento to have a special pair of shoes fitted with braces. Well, one night while getting him ready for a bath I undressed him and said, 'Okay, go get in the tub.'

"As he walked away from me I noticed when his hip reached a plumb line with his ankle it would twist. That told me that was due to alignment and that he, then, was just twisting his foot right off his shoe.

"After seeing this, I told my wife, 'You take that boy to Doc André.' She said, 'Well Dr. R. says he needs new shoes.' I said, 'If you don't take him, I'm going to.'

"She said, 'All right. I'll take him.' Dr. André gave him a treatment and told my wife to bring him back in two days. In less than a week's time, he was all straightened out.

"Shortly thereafter, I was blasting stumps on an extremely hot day. I must have inhaled a whiff of the nitro powder because all of a sudden I got sick.

"I got so sick I didn't think I could make it to the house. I went into the house to get cleaned up to go to Dr. André's place. I did manage to get my face and hands washed before I passed out.

"Well, somehow, the family got me into the car, but before they could get me to Dr. André's, I passed out again! Lord, I was sick! My wife, Lois, was scared to death!

"She got us to the doctor's place, ran down the path, and got Dr. André. He and Lois managed to get me into the treatment room where he lifted me onto one of the tables.

"Dr. André was a powerful man and I only weighed about 145 pounds at that time. He asked what had I done. Lois told him she didn't really know other than I'd been blasting out some old stumps on our property.

"The doctor started working on me until I came to. He said I never would have made it into Placerville to a regular doctor or the hospital (10 miles away), because the nitro powder was very toxic. He said it could have paralyzed my liver in that amount of time. Now whether this is true or not, I don't know, but that's exactly what he said. This was the only time I ever wondered if Dr. André knew what he was talking about.

"I feel he did the right thing because I was able to walk out of there. I still felt deathly sick when I got home, and suffered the rest of the afternoon, but I was able to work the next day."   **O. Beckett**

"In 1944, I owned a motel in Placerville. People always asked for directions to Dr. André's place. I remember a man telling his story of working on a sign on a roof.

"He stepped back and went through the sheet rock. Later, a bump appeared on his right hand. One doctor said it could be cancer. After three radiation treatments, the man refused to go back.

"He went to Dr. André who ran his thumb between the man's shoulders. It was very painful. He told the man to put a small, solid, square pillow on his back and then push against a corner of a chair.   After several days, the bump went away."   **A. McFarland**

"One day, my dad was going past the André's place on his way to work.   He was a logger for Morton's Mill.

"This one day he stopped to talk to Frank who was getting ready to butcher a goat.   He watched as the doctor reached down with one hand, picked up a good-sized goat, and lifted it up over the fence.   He was a very strong man.   This really impressed the other loggers when I told them about it."   **R. Neilsen**

"The owner of the Michigan Cal Lumber Mill during WWII would take the company bus down to Sacramento to Second Street.   Loggers and those looking for work would hang out there.

"Sometimes they would be in such bad shape he would send a bunch of them out to the Goat Doctor's to get straightened up before they went to work."

W. Swansborough

"He saved my life!

"During World War II, while working under a bomber at McClellan Field in Sacramento, a bomb door dropped open and hit me in the head.   I had horrible headaches and a lot of pain in my back and in my hip.   I went to several doctors who could find nothing wrong, even after taking X-rays.

"I went to the Goat Doctor.   I didn't tell him what was wrong because he didn't ask.   He put his hands on me, feeling my spine, and then massaged it.   He didn't massage hard.   Then he felt my neck.   On one side of my neck, he pressed a spot with his thumb.

"Suddenly I heard a kind of buzzing or ringing sound in my head and could feel pressure being released and my headache went away. My back, hip and head felt immediately better.

"When he was finished, he explained to me that my relief was only temporary and that I should see a medical doctor. I went to two or three doctors. They did tests and could not find anything wrong with me.

"When I felt bad again I went back to him. He gave me the same treatment and again told me to find a medical doctor. When I told him I had, and they said nothing was wrong with me, he said, 'Then find a different one.'

"I went to the Goat Doctor about every six months for two years. Each time, he would again insist, that I be seen by a medical doctor.

"Finally, I saw a physician who checked me and found that I had a brain tumor. He did surgery and I've been fine ever since. I never would have thought of a brain tumor.

"I think he might have been a faith healer or maybe he did what they do today called pressure point healing. Dr. André was real quiet, but he didn't really have time to talk with people—he was always so busy.

"Everything was clean and he was very clean. His hands were like magic. He was just one 'wonderful man'." **I. Radonich**

"I was at the Goat Doctor's place the very day Lettie Forni and her friend were killed while on their way to see him.

"He was really a different gentleman, very kind and soft spoken, and soft touching. It was a different experience, I'll tell you. People who went to him thought he could do no wrong, absolutely thought he could cure anything." **B. Cola**

"They found Mrs. Forni's car a day after the mishap. It had plunged 80 feet over the grade into the American River and was submerged in water. They didn't have the dams we have now and the water was much deeper. My father, Orval, went down under the water to connect a cable to the car in order to pull it out." **D. Beckett**

"Around 1946, I took my friend Vera to see the Goat Doctor just before she was due for an operation.

"She was in so much pain from a twisted pelvic which also caused her left knee problems.

"When the Goat Doctor asked me if I loved my friend, I said, 'Yes.' He showed me how to twist and roll Vera. He said to do this for ten days straight. Vera walked out of the doctor's office—no operation was necessary." **L. Rivard**

"As a little girl, I heard the Goat Doctor's name often. My grandfather was a regular patient, finding relief from perpetual back pain. My father was taken there in 1947, as a young man with blinding migraine headaches.

"'I remember the Goat Doctor's hair the most,' my Dad said. 'He would lay you upon a crude table, which was covered with goatskins. This is where he worked on you. I don't know why, but he could cure the pain when nothing else would work. I would find relief from the pain for several months before I would need to return. I went to him for several years. The worst part of a visit to the Goat Doctor was the long wait. I remember when it was hot, dry, and dusty. There would be people lined up forever.'"

P. Presba - Georgetown Gazette

"We would come up to get treatments during 1945, 46, and 47. I had been a cowboy and my back was troublesome. The cartilage had grown wrong because the vertebrae had never been realigned.

"Dr. André had to release all the old problems before he could begin to adjust. He fixed me up fine."

G. Bottenberg

"This old lady used to sit in a rocker in the doorway of the Goat Doctor's cabin, holding something that looked like a small dowsing rod.

"Hanging from what appeared to be a length of wood, about the size of a pencil, was a wood or metal ball attached by a string, which was either the same length or a little shorter than the rod.

"As people came down the path, they'd see her with this rod in her hand. It would be moving this way and that. Then she'd tell the Goat Doctor what was wrong with them. You can't imagine how accurate she was."

Doc Almond

"Dr. André told my brother-in-law how to make a small dowsing rod. He showed him how to hold it over food. He said it would swing one way if the food was good for him and another if it was not."

E. Kamp

"I saw Frank about six times from the forties to the early 1950's. A friend had to drive me, as my back was so bad. I received some relief. The road was not paved, very narrow and not for the timid soul.

"I recall that Frank began closing practice at 5:00 p.m. to rest, help care for the animals and sometimes work in the garden.

"It was word of mouth — hearsay, that I heard of his mother using a dowsing rod. I heard he belonged to the Rosicrucian Society. I thought him to be a bit eccentric."   **J. Hatton**

"Mother André was psychic–she didn't need a dowsing rod or any such thing."   **C. Neilsen**

"I lived with my Uncle in Mosquito for about three years when I was in my late teens. He lived about two miles from the Goat Doctor on what was called Misery Hill.

"I'd go past his place on my way to visit my girlfriend.

"I remember Carmelita coming out to greet me and handing me a couple of pears. The Andrés never failed in letting me know I was welcome to stop in any time I was near-by.

"Whenever I did, they always invited me in for food and drink immediately upon seeing me. Even after moving from the area, I was to make frequent trips to and from Mosquito for ten years.

"I drove up there to visit my uncle one day. He had become well acquainted with the Goat Doctor by then and I saw that he had a couple of goats running around. Dr. André had convinced him of the benefits one could expect if their diet contained goat milk.

"The first time my uncle offered me a glass of goat milk, I darn near threw up. It was so different. Just the smell of it was disgusting.

"On each recurring visit to my uncle's place, I noticed he had a couple more goats, until finally he had six or eight. Each time there, he'd offer me a little more of his goat products. Not to be rude or hurt his feelings, I'd have a little. This became a little more each time, until I grew to like it. Now, I can't think of ever tasting any cottage cheese or butter as good as that made from fresh goat milk, it's delicious!

"My uncle had a medical problem. He wasn't one to complain or to discuss his troubles, so I didn't know what his problem was. He went to see Dr. André.

"The doctor put my uncle on a grape diet, seeds and all. People thought it a ridiculous diet, but my uncle believed in Dr. André, so he did as he said.

"My uncle was in his late sixties at the time he started the grape diet. He continued on it until he died at age 98. I found out later, my uncle's medical problem was Cancer." **J. Perona**

"We lived in north Sacramento in the 40's. My dad worked every day of his life to care for us six children. My mother made our clothes from the sacks that the chicken and cow feed came in. We grew almost everything we ate. The point is we had no money to spend on foolish things.

"My parents thought it important enough for us kids to have an occasional checkup and to spend five dollars for the care of five of us. My father liked to donate $1 per child so whoever was the healthiest stayed home.

"The night before our trip, my mom would stay up late and make lunch for us all. My aunt, uncle, and two cousins came early in the morning—long before daylight. We all piled into my uncle's car with younger children sitting on the laps of the older ones. Off we would head towards Placerville. In those days, it seemed a million miles away. By the time we arrived at our destination, the sun was barely rising over the mountains.

"Multitudes of people lined the trails as far as we could see. The line moved very slowly. We sat down and ate our lunch when the sun was overhead. My

Uncle stood in line while we all ate so we could keep our place in line. The first one finished took his place so he could eat. It was still morning, but it seemed like a full day. There were other children and we all played a game of tag to pass the time away.

"Finally, we were down the trail. I could see the old mountain cabin with farm animals running around in the yard. As we drew closer to the cabin, I decided I didn't want to go in. My mother assured me there was nothing to fear. As I stepped through the doorway, I was greeted by a dark complexioned lady in buckskin clothing. Her hair was long and black. She motioned for me to crawl up on a wooden table covered with animal skins.

"Suddenly I looked up and behind me stood a man with long hair wearing a buckskin shirt. He had an omniscient aura about him. I was sure I was in the presence of Jesus. I was so tense, but he assured me it was okay to relax. He began to move his hands over my head and shoulders.

"He asked if I had had a fall. I had fallen out of a tree sometime before. After a while, he told me he was done. I climbed off the table and went out the door.

"By the time we were on the road to home, the sun was going down. It had been a long day, one I would never forget. This was the Goat Doctor through the eyes of a child."   **J. Colvard**

"We lived about seven miles from the Goat Doctor. There were always tons of cars in front of his place. I remember seeing cars from Florida, New York, and Pennsylvania. If you didn't bring food, you would about starve to death! It was such a long wait.

"I had a fifteen-year old friend who had polio and limped badly. We got her mother's permission to take her over to see the doctor.

"He found one leg to be a few inches shorter than the other one. He gave her an adjustment and told her to rub something on her leg, (I don't remember what it was) and to soak it with a hot wet towel every day. Within months, her leg grew two inches.

"I remember his smiling a lot with very gentle eyes."

"My mother had a very bad back. He told her he wanted to see her again after her first treatment. I remember Dr. André telling her to heat a stove lid, wrap it in paper and a towel, and put it on the small of her back while riding to his place.

"I was very, very thin and his mother told my mother to give me a half glass of beer each day. My mother couldn't go along with this."   **J. Dixon**

"Our daughter was born with cerebral palsy. We did not know this until she was two-and-a-half-years old, as she did not show signs of it.

"The doctors did not diagnose it as such. At one-and-a-half, she could not sit up straight in her high chair to eat. We had to tie her in. She did feed herself.

"Following her first treatment from Dr. André, she sat up on a step stool and ate her meal. I was so excited I could hardly eat! Dr. André showed us some stretch exercises to do for our daughter, which we did faithfully.

"We did take her a few more times. Each time we could see improvements. She learned to walk fairly well.

"As a person, he had the most kind eyes and hands. If one has an image of Christ—that would be Dr. André." **P. Walters**

"When I was ten years of age, I took a bad fall down a hill. For three weeks, I could not walk unaided. My mother took me to various doctors who checked me thoroughly.

"Even after having done a spinal tap, they told her nothing was wrong with me. My mother said this was ridiculous because she saw how much pain I was in.

"She told the doctors there was absolutely no reason for me to pretend to be in pain and to act like a cripple, especially, since before the accident, I had always been psychologically a very happy child.

"We lived in Richmond, California at the time. Thankfully, someone told my mother of the Goat Doctor. Along with my aunt and uncle, my mother and I made the dangerous trek to Mosquito. This was about 1947. I still remember how scary it felt when we finally got there. People were all over the place.

"I remember being carried into the waiting room. The room was full of people sitting and laying around on the floor waiting their turn.

"If you ever visited the Goat Doctor's clinic, you would never forget it. It was all so spooky inside the cabin. The rooms were small and somewhat dark like a cave.

"When my turn came, I was carried into his treatment room and put on a long table. I remember the doctor walking up behind me to the head of the table.

"He first put his hands on my head and then my shoulders, doing some kind of minor adjustment. After doing the same gentle procedure to my neck and hip area, he told me to stand, and I did. Then he told me to walk in a way that assured me I could, and I did!

"At one point during the course of the treatment, my mother started to talk to the doctor. I remember him putting a finger up to his mouth, motioning to her to be quiet.

"When done, he told my mother that I came close to having a broken neck. While there, I watched several other people being carried in and walk out."

W. Dortzbach

"I heard of him when I was working for the water district. I had been in an accident and couldn't walk. I had not walked for two years. I had been seen by two chiropractors.

"I was in misery all the way up there. I had such back pain in the sciatic nerve. He said my backbone had slipped off the pelvic bone.

"He gave a pull and there was a snap that sounded like someone had stuck a pin in a balloon. I only went there two times. The first treatment did it. The second was just a checkup and gentle massage. He really helped me out.

"He saw my wife also. She had very bad migraine headaches since she was a girl. He told her she had been in a car accident. He was right!" **M. Clark**

"I first went to the Goat Doctor with a couple of friends who went there for treatment. I went out of curiosity.

"Years later, while living in Fallon, Nevada, my husband was working in a shop at the old airbase rebuilding large plane engines. He lifted a crate that was too heavy and popped his sacroiliac. He couldn't straighten up. We drove to our friend's house in Placerville with him in that condition.

"Our friend took my husband to Dr. André. Dr. André said it was too soon to work on him. He told my husband to go back to our friend's, buy a belladonna pack, and keep it on his back.

"He did this, then, went back to Dr. André. One treatment did the trick; my husband was fine.

"I remember he always stopped at noon for lunch – no matter how many people were waiting." **B. Tyler**

"My father took me to the Goat Doctor when I was about 10 years of age. I had Wyres Syndrome.

"He did soft manipulation to my neck, which made it feel better. He told me he couldn't heal me. I remember his clothes smelled like sheep dip and his breath of garlic, but he was one of the nicest men you could ever want to meet." **G. Lay**

"I was 38 years old when I contracted polio. I spent several months in a hospital, paralyzed on the right side. My stomach and bladder would not work for three weeks and bowels for two months.

"Two very good friends, John Buck, a non-believer in most things, and Lowell West, were very much in favor of Dr. André. When I heard that from John, I decided to go out to see him. This was about nine months after my attack of polio.

"I was on Canadian crutches. I worked in the basement of the post office. I would creep up each stair with each foot. After the first treatment, I began to improve. Soon, I was walking from the post office to the courthouse across the street with a cane. I definitely credit Dr. André with my recovery and ability to continue to work.

"One time in the waiting room, a big man was helped down the hill. He was walking on his hands and feet he was so bent over. Dr. André asked if those waiting would mind and he took this man in first. Not much later, the man came out flexing his muscles and walking upright.

"A friend of ours turned yellow with jaundice and went to Dr. André. He turned her upside down and put her on the back of her head then gently rotated her. He emptied her gall bladder and she recovered quickly.

"Another friend was told, by a neurologist in Sacramento that he had spine bending and that he would eventually become permanently bent way over. He was in lots of pain.

"He went to Dr. André and as the adjustment was progressing, there was a very sharp pain in one section of the chest area and then he was fine. He lived to be 85 and never became bent over.

"He said a great deal of his power came from his hair and that's why he never cut it. Others said they heard him say it was from chastity.

"I always felt that Dr. André reminded me of the Lord—strength and love together. He once told me *'The public knows only its own pain.'*   **B. Maguire**

"I remember when a family from the Merced or Modesto area brought their daughter of about nine or ten to the Goat Doctor. She could not walk and the parents had been told there was no hope. She was left with the Andrés for three weeks. When the father and mother returned, they saw their little girl jumping rope in the yard."   **C. Henningsen**

"In 1946-47, we lived in Cedar Grove, California. I was twelve years old. I had taken a fall one day while roller-skating backwards. I could hardly walk. I was taken on the most horrible road to see a man called the Goat Doctor.

"There was a long line of cars on each side of the road and a cabin down in a gully. We waited all day long.

"It was all kind of scary until I got into the cabin and the doctor spoke to me. He was the most wonderful man. I don't know what he did, but it didn't hurt. When he was done, I walked out as though I'd never had an accident.

"Things that stand out in my memories of him are that I always think of him as the original hippie and how immaculate he was."   **M. Scalzi**

"In 1946 or 1947, my father was a truck driver. All the truckers he knew used to go to the Goat Doctor when they had back trouble. He did a wonderful job on my father.

"My father said he had heard some derogatory things about him, but he was in awe of the man. He always left him five dollars, which in those days was a lot of money. He was always so happy to feel good again.

"He treated my mother at one point. I remember she had on a skirt. He covered her legs with a sheet. Dr. André was so friendly and had such a gentle manner.

"It always took at least a full day when we went there. We would buy what we called a party pack—a loaf of Wonder Bread and a package of bologna. My brothers and I played tag and ran all over the place."   **T. Dorsey**

"I did not meet him until the winter of 1947. As a draftsman, I was stationed in Placerville to draw original maps of the town for the new route for Highway 50. There were two survey parties supplying me with the topography data.

"I had hurt my back real bad and the pain was killing me. I could barely get in and out of my Jeep. One morning while in Placerville, I happened to stop at a service station. The truck stop was a great gathering spot for truck drivers.

"One of the truckers helped me out of the Jeep and invited me in for coffee. On seeing my condition, the men began telling me about the Goat Doctor.

"At least six of them started giving me a bad time because I didn't want to go to him, but after listening to several of their testimonies about him I decided to pay a visit.

"It was eight miles down into the American River canyon to his home. There was about a foot and a half of snow on the ground and the road was very icy, but I made it.

"There were several people there who had carpooled from Los Angeles. There was a big pile of cut wood in the front yard, chickens, and about 30 to 40 goats all around the cabin.

"Dr. André invited me to come into the cabin. It was dark inside. He wore Levis, a shirt, and slippers. I marveled at his long, gray hair that was braided and hung over his belt.

"He was soft-spoken and almost feminine in his speech and manner. He asked me why I was there and I told him. He then directed me to a table. I wondered what was going to happen.

"Here he was, only five-foot three or five-foot four-inches tall, and maybe one hundred-thirty to one hundred-forty pounds and I was six-foot two and weighed two-hundred ten pounds!

"However, it didn't take me long to discover that he was equal to the job, I was really surprised.

"He checked the position of my feet then went to the head of the table where he stepped on a small box.

He put a half-nelson hold on my head and shoulders and began rocking me back and forth.

"All of a sudden, he gave me an awful twist to the right and then to the left. He again checked my feet then had me hang my legs over the side of the table. Then he kind of shook them until I relaxed and then jerked them and straightened everything out.

"He worked on me for about thirty minutes. He then had me lay down on a cot for about an hour with a hot water bottle in various locations and then back to the table for a repetition of the first exercises. He said that was all he could do for now. I donated either two dollars or two dollars and fifty cents.

"He treated my wife for a neck injury that he said happened in her childhood. He was right. It had bothered her for years. He helped her with one treatment.

"Thus began a long and thankful relationship. I wish he were still here. He pulled me out of a few bad times." **M. Coburn**

"I remember the Goat Doctor as a very humble person. Many people from our town of Winters made regular pilgrimages to Mosquito. Most of the people were desperate to get his medical help." **N. Santos**

"We were living in Jackson at the time, when my mother began having severe muscle spasms in her back. My mother was a very skeptical person, but finally in desperation and having heard so many people talk positive about the Goat Doctor, she decided to pay him a visit.

"I, of course, had to go with her. This was the way it was with my mother. Every thing she did, I had to do. If she had a stomachache and had to take one or two antacid tablets, I had to take one or two antacid tablets. I was still a young girl when we started paying visits to Dr. André due to my mother's bad back.

"My mother and I had come from Vienna when I was only four, so it was especially nice to hear Dr. André talk as he was from Vienna also, and spoke with a slight accent. He was so charming. He had a very pleasant voice and sounded well educated.

"We visited him often, until one day he said to my mother, 'My dear Mrs., I can fix your back, but the rough road you have to take home will always undo most of what I have done. You can fix your back yourself. Let me give you some instructions on exercising that will strengthen your back and make it well.'

"The exercises were so good that not only did her back get completely well and strong, her varicose veins improved immensely. She had always had to wear thick elastic stockings.

"After a while of doing the exercises, she noticed her veins were smaller and her legs felt so good that she no longer needed the elastic stockings. He was generous to a fault."   **A. Carleton**

"I remember Dr. André. He helped my husband when he fell off a platform while with the Southern Pacific Railroad. That was about 1948.

"When my sister, Violet, hurt her back while lifting a heavy box, she was in real pain. She came to stay with us in Clarksburg. We took her to three chiropractors, but they didn't help. We took her to a bone specialist. He wanted to operate and it would leave her with a stiff hip joint. She said, 'No.'

"Then, one evening my husband and I were wondering what to do next when we thought of the Goat Doctor. We asked her, and she said, 'Yes.' So, my brother and my husband helped her downstairs and took her to Dr. André.

"They waited for her and my husband said, 'Out she came with a big smile on her face and tears rolling down her cheeks.' She was just fine! He was one wonderful doctor."   **C. Shaw**

"My family first went to Dr. Andrés in the forties. We lived in Stockton at the time. We would have to leave our home very early in the day. I was sixteen years of age and remember being scared to death just thinking about going on that horrible road.

"My father had built a platform, of sorts, to hook my mother's heavy and cumbersome wheelchair to the back bumper of our 1936 Ford Sedan. Every time we would hit a bump or make a sharp turn, my father liked to tease my mother that she was going to lose her wheels!

"My mother had multiple sclerosis. We had taken her to many other doctors with no positive results. It was kind of a last ditch effort, when upon hearing of the Goat Doctor, my father decided to give him a try.

"Dr. André told my father he could make my mother feel better, but that he could not cure her. After her treatment, he told my father to bring her back in four or five weeks and to come to the back door and knock and he would take my mother right in. Each visit brought my mother four or five days of relief.

"Dr. André always greeted us with a big smile. He absolutely radiated warmth. It never mattered if he had a problem. He was just a super nice person. He became very dear to us. He was our friend.

"Never, but never, would he take a penny from us.

"Instead, he always sent us home with vegetables from his garden. Even after telling him we had our own vegetable garden, he insisted we take some of his.

"We were to make the trek to Dr. André's place at least thirty times, as patients and as friends. We would have gone more often, except we couldn't get through the roads in the wintertime."   **J. Roberts**

"One day, a girl was brought in on a stretcher. When Frank became aware of her being carried along the path, he told those already inside to wait.

"He went to the door and stood and watched as they came closer. He told those carrying her to bring her right in. She was inside barely ten minutes and he corrected the problem."   **E. Teany**

"While surveying for the Bureau of Reclamation at Sly Park Dam I developed a very bad neck and back problem and went to the Goat Doctor.

"I remember waiting all day. There were many people from all over the country.

"I was amazed at the immediate relief after one adjustment. In one treatment I was able to carry my surveying equipment without stress."   **J. Baldwin**

"We lived in San Francisco and my little boy was extremely lame. I took him to the Children's Hospital and they told me they would have to put him in a cast from waist down.

"He would be in a sitting position for six months and then in a walking brace. I was just sick. I told my husband, 'I'm going up to see mama before they put him in a cast as we won't be able to do much traveling after.' Mama said, 'Why don't you take him out to see Dr. André?' So we ran him out there.

"Dr. André looked him over real good and said, 'I don't see any major problem here.' He then did what he called a gentle massage on his little spine for about 10 minutes.

"We were there on a Thursday and Dr. André had us come again and repeated the treatment on Friday. He wanted to see my boy again on Sunday morning. Again, he did just a few minutes of what appeared to be gentle manipulation or massage on him.

"When we took our boy back to the Children's Hospital the doctor who checked him, looked at him and said, 'This boy doesn't need a brace!'

"I tell you, that man did some marvelous things."

J. Richards

"While working for the Michigan-Cal Lumber Company, I slipped on the green lumber and tore the hip cartilage. A medical doctor treated me but was of no help. So I told the doctor, I was going out to see the Goat Doctor. 'He can't help you,' the doctor said.

"Dr. André checked me and found a one-inch difference in the length on my legs, so he did an adjustment. Then he did a technique of placing a pillow between my shoulder blades while I was sitting on the edge of the table, hands clasped behind my head. Then he wove his arms in front my arms and locked his hands together. He put his knee on the pillow, and with a short and easy movement, he pulled up with his arms and pushed into the pillow with his knee at the same time. You could hear the vertebrae move all the way down my upper back.

"Dr. André told me when they first came to Mosquito he had a very extensive case of poison oak and his mother buried him in a dirt trench fully naked for a half day to cure him. He said when he came out of the dirt his poison oak was all gone and never came back.

"Dr. André told us that for continuing aches and pains, we should bury our bare feet in dirt for half an hour morning and night."   **B. Waggersman**

"As a pedestrian, my sister had to jump out of the way of an oncoming car. In doing so, she injured herself and couldn't walk. Her husband took her to the Goat Doctor and had to carry her in. She was in there for just a few minutes and walked out—never another problem."   **M. Mainwaring**

"Frank was a very amazing man. While working at Beeches Mill, I threw a vertebra out in my back while piling lumber. I went to him as most all the men did at one time or another."   **M. VeerKamp**

"Whenever my Dad had a back problem, he headed for the Goat Doctor's place, as many of his coworkers at the East Lawn Funeral Home in Sacramento did.

"When I had what turned out to be a pinched nerve, my parents took me to see him. On my tenth birthday, he gave me a goatskin rug, which I treasured for years. He was such a kind, soft-spoken man."   **C. Smith**

"I was there one day for treatment, sitting on one of the benches lining the walls of the front porch-like area, which was full. The windows looked up the hill and I could see the road above.

"About mid-morning another car stopped on the road. A couple got out and then helped a young man out and into a wheelchair. With the help from some men, they got him down to the waiting room.

"Dr. André came from the treatment room and asked if we would mind waiting for these folks, who had come a long way. The young man had been paralyzed for a couple of years from a football accident. No doctors were able to help him.

"About one hour later the door opened and the young man, aided by his parents, walked out. They were crying tears of joy and we in the waiting room were crying, too."   **T. Boldt**

"Since I was a child, I have heard of the Goat Doctor. One of my cousins was stricken with crippling arthritis and confined to a wheelchair shortly after the birth of her one and only daughter.

"My aunt and uncle, took her to numerous doctors and finally to the man known as the Goat Doctor. He prescribed for her to drink goat milk.

"I recently spoke to one of her sisters and asked if the milk was of any help to her. She said her sister claimed it did make her feel better, but she herself thought it was because that was what her sister wanted to believe."   **M. Gregorio**

"For years, my father couldn't hold a job because he was so sick with asthma. Finally, in the late 40's, he got so ill he almost died. The allergy specialist, who had been treating him, had given up. It was he who sent my father to the Goat Doctor.

"The Goat Doctor recommended my father be put on goat's milk. The other thing that he had my father do was to take some kind of honey. My father bought a goat, which I used to milk. I drank goat's milk in those days and I believe this is why I have compliments on my skin today."   **J. Kludjian**

"Lack of water contributes to asthma. If you don't have enough water in your system, the body draws water from the lungs."   **Frank André**

"Although he had a shack for a house and he looked like a hermit. The man was fantastic.

"I had polio when I was three. He would manipulate my spine and make me feel better."

L. Hess

"Our neighbor used to have a stand at the Farmer's Public Market on Twelve and J Street in Sacramento selling herbs and vitamins.

"I know the Goat Doctor bought a lot of herbs from him and he would go to Mosquito every two or three weeks with a delivery, and to pick some herb called Mountain Misery that grew up there.

"After the Mountain Misery dried, you let it steep in water and sip about a tablespoon of it and it really perks you up. Dr. André also received deliveries from a pharmaceutical company."

A. Hess

"Frank use to ship a lot of Mountain Misery all over the country to people."

P. DeWolfe

"I knew a paratrooper during the war. He suffered quite a bit. He was in horrible pain. He couldn't do anything but stand or lay down.

"He said he didn't know what the Goat Doctor did other than he went behind him and said a prayer; he was immediately well.

"There was a long line of cars, even limousines but he never rushed. He met a woman and that was his downfall."

T. Fujii

"I made a number of trips to see this amazing man. I'm sure he had a license to operate but who cared when your back was killing you. His long hair and long beard made him look like Jesus Christ.

"His very simple mountain home was his place of business. When your turn came to be manipulated, he had you lay on a plain wooden table covered with goatskins.

"Talking was not one of his virtues. He said little and asked less. He didn't want you to tell him what was wrong with your back. His fingers and hands did all the walking and talking.

"His treatments were so very fast and effective. It was hard to believe, but he was a "Miracle Worker" indeed. The cost was $3.00 a visit and you laid the money on the desk. He would not touch it while we were there.

"One couple I met had brought an eleven-year-old girl for a treatment after all others failed. The family said she would not be walking today if it weren't for the Goat Doctor.

"A short ride out of Placerville made it a good trip, but after a visit with the Goat Doctor, the return trip to Placerville was more pleasant than ever because I had no pain."   **T. Budnik**

"I had permission from Frank to hunt for deer on his property anytime during hunting season. A friend and I were around a glowing campfire after an unsuccessful day of hunting. My friend decided to play Taps on his always-handy trumpet.

"Within a few minutes, Frank was by our side with a big grin, saying he had heard our beautiful music and just thought he'd let us know that a mountain lion had killed one of his goats nearby, a day or two before, so we weren't apt to find any deer thereabouts. The deer would stay clear of the area for several weeks at least, because of the smell of death.

"Frank sat by the campfire visiting awhile. Then, as he was about to leave, my friend said, 'Don't forget to turn your clock back an hour.' Frank said he never set his clock ahead. He always kept it on standard time and saw no sense in changing it.

"He said he couldn't understand why the whole country had to set their clocks back and forth—just because a few people couldn't figure out how to get up an hour earlier or later as need be." **Don Thompsen**

"I have only good memories of the Goat Doctor.

"The last time I visited him was in 1952. I had bent over to lift a sack of cement out of the kids' wagon. I felt my back pop and I couldn't straighten.

"I had to put my hand under my leg to raise the right foot to put it on the gas and the brake pedals. I was so bent over the people in the waiting room took one look at me and said, 'Oh you better go in ahead of us.'

"His heavy-duty table was covered with a piece of canvas and several pieces of rope to tie across your legs to keep you from falling off. I hurt for several days after but didn't have to go back."   **C. Otis**

"I worked on a ranch and while loading a truck, I put my back out. I went to different doctors in Sacramento. They said I needed surgery and there was only a 50/50 chance of it doing any good. I wasn't going to let anyone operate on my back!

"The Goat Doctor put me on a long table like the doctors use. I was in terrible pain. He didn't massage my back vigorously at all. In fact, I could barely feel his hands. He was so gentle.

"I was taking a prescription of morphine, or some pain killer, three and four times a week before he took care of me in one treatment of maybe 30 minutes.

"He was very popular. There were many people lined up waiting in cars. He was a very quiet and gentle man. He looked just like Jesus." **A. Tsujimoto**

"To begin with, the reason that I was in need of help dated back to December 17, 1951, just before my 18th birthday, when I was struck down by a hit-and-run drunk driver.

"I landed on my head about twenty feet from point of impact and slid in gravel. A motorist and his family who witnessed the accident had to speed up to 85 miles per hour just to get close enough to read the license plate and then came back to help me.

"Before I was ever picked up off the ground, my left hip (point of impact) had swelled out about six inches and down my hip about ten inches.

"That hip received two operations, one to remove a long calcium deposit and when the swelling continued down the hip, a tumor had to be removed, both the result of the impact. I finally had to have the hip replaced, but because of the prior surgeries and the surgeon used the wrong size implant, it wasn't all that successful.

"I, also, had a fractured pelvis and many other injuries. I was told, had the impact been just one eighth of an inch closer to my spine, I would have been totally paralyzed or killed outright.

"After eight surgeries relating to that accident, I'm really perturbed that drunk drivers are still getting away relatively punishment free. He was fined three hundred and fifty dollars and I got a life sentence, because the trauma to my body has come back to haunt me as I get older.

"Before I heard of the Goat Doctor, I was experiencing great back pain and difficulty in walking unaided. I had several sessions with a licensed chiropractor who used ultra sound.

"He advised my parents that I would need approximately 135 treatments, at a minimum of $20.00 each, which my parents could ill afford. At any rate, neither the chiropractor nor his treatments impressed me at all, so I refused to go back.

"By the summer of 1953, it had become extremely difficult for me to get around. I was in pain all the time. Friends of my fiancé kept telling me of a man they referred to as a "healer" who was called the "Goat Doctor."

"Having been less than impressed by the chiropractor, I was highly skeptical of the things I was hearing about the Goat Doctor. Some of the things I heard were quite unbelievable to me and I scoffed at them as highly improbable. At the time, I was 19 years old.

"I heard from people who had been treated by Mr. André, that he reminded them of the images they had seen of Jesus. He was described to me as having a beard and long gray hair, which he wore in a single braid which hung down his back.

"They, also, told me that he rarely spoke to his patients but helped them immensely. Some of these friends are California Indians and they were absolutely convinced that Mr. André was a true healer. They persuaded me that I had nothing to lose by asking him for help.

"The process of getting to see Mr. André was on a first come, first serve basis, which seemed to work very well. When we arrived at about eleven in the evening, there were already 22 cars ahead of our group, which consisted of several cars.

"We camped out overnight and everyone pretty much chatted all night. I might add that no one tried to push to the front of the line as some people do.

"The next morning, Saturday, I noticed one young man who I would say was in his early thirties. He was extremely well built and muscular, but his right arm was locked in an odd position. It was almost straight out from the shoulder but bent at the elbow.

"He told me he was unable to move it. Being 19 and a true skeptic, I tried my best to move that arm but couldn't budge it. He told me that he had been to all sorts of doctors all over the United States, but no one had been able to help him.

"Another man, perhaps a little younger, had a hump as large as a soccer ball on his back. This hump, when I felt it, was a hard as a rock. I didn't see how anything could help that.

"He and his parents told me that he had been all over the world trying to get help. His parents had spent thousands of dollars to no avail. He was almost without any hope of ever being cured.

"I was naturally very curious to see the outcome of their treatment. I was stunned when the man with the bent arm came out swinging his arm and crying like a baby, but a very happy one. He was all smiles and jubilant.

"The young man who went in with the large hump on his back also came out crying and laughing at the same time. The hump had virtually disappeared except for a very slight mound perhaps a quarter of an inch high.

"I would never have noticed it had I not seen and felt the hump before he went in. He was told to come back on the following Saturday for another treatment.

"After seeing these two recovered, I began to have some hope for myself. There were of course, many other people, who had treatments that morning, but I would have to say that the recovery of the two young men impressed me the most.

"The slope from the service road above the house was rather steep for someone with difficulty walking, and for some reason, I lost my footing and literally ran down the hill.

"I crashed into the fence around the vegetable garden and had to be helped up. The people I was with were able to fix the fence, but I was extremely embarrassed about the incident and hesitant about going in for my treatment.

"Mr. André motioned for me to sit in the straight backed chair and started running his fingers up and down my back. His touch was so gentle I could barely feel it.

"Having heard that he rarely spoke to anyone, I was quite surprised when he asked me if I had been in some sort of accident.

"When I told him of being struck down by a speeding car, he told me that every vertebra in my back was out of place. He worked on me for about twenty minutes, and then told me to lie flat on my back on a wooden table for another twenty minutes. If my memory is correct, the treatment table was in the far right corner against the wall. The chair was sort of in the middle of the room.

"While I was on my back on the table, Mr. André worked on some of the others who came with me. He then worked on me for about another twenty minutes, using a gentle touching of his fingers all over my back. He then said I should feel better.

"For almost twenty years after that, I had no trouble walking and only got backaches from lifting heavy loads of paper. I worked in the bindery at McClellan AFB for 20 years as a collator operator, which involved lifting thousands of pounds of paper every day.

"The treatment Mr. André gave to me was perhaps one of the best things that could have happened to me in my entire lifetime. My only regret is that he has passed away, because if he were still alive, I couldn't get there quickly enough!

"Mr. André wore clean blue coveralls and a blue work shirt. I can assure you that he certainly did not have the odor of "goat" about him.

"He was neat and clean, and the fact that he could perform the magic he performed just by using a light touch of his fingers, was to me truly amazing then, and even more so now, considering all the equipment that chiropractors use today in their fancy treatment rooms.

"Mr. André, on the other hand would not accept a dime more that three dollars from anyone. The fee was the same regardless of the length of time it took for him to help a person. Many people, including me, offered him more money, but to no avail. That in itself is amazing.

"Mr. André is a man that I met only once, but can never forget. I would have to believe that his healing powers were truly a gift from God. Nothing I have seen before or since has impressed me the way he did."
                                                    W. Denson

"One time, my mother had a bad back and I drove her to him. I was driving a 1948 Willy's Jeep and every time I hit a bump, my mother hollered out in pain. My mother couldn't even walk—I had to carry her in.

"I remember the place as not very clean and rather dark and dingy. He was wearing a not-so-white robe type affair. I'm not sure if he dressed that way to emulate the impression of Jesus or not.

"My mother remarked how he looked like Jesus Christ. I said I didn't know what Jesus looked like. My mother felt he had a spiritual touch and way about him. After thirty minutes, my mother came out walking and has been fine ever since.

"He was a humble person and I believe all the stories about him. He was definitely not a myth."

W. Weichold

"I had real bad headaches from tumbling. My parents took me to doctors who gave me all kinds of tests. They even did an encephalogram and spinal tap.

"It cost my parents a fortune and I still had headaches so they took me to Dr. André for a treatment.

"He was wearing a white robe, like a biblical character. I remember his hands were big and gentle. I am in my sixties now and have never had a headache since."

D. Johns

"I was teethed on Goat Doctor stories."

R. Rminger

"I was a ski instructor at the Rainbow Lodge, Donner area. I went to the Goat Doctor around 1952-53 after a friend said the Veterans Administrations Office sent him there. His injury was healed.

"I had been injured and left with a paralyzed arm. He didn't talk to me my first visit there. He wore no shirt and no shoes, had long hair and piercing dark eyes.

"On my second trip there, my brother-in-law counted nine different out-of-state car licenses! It was all first come, first served. He had one person evidently being relaxed on a cot with hot water bottles and had two treatment tables with people on them. He told one to rest a minute or two and then worked on the other. It was unbelievable! People just stood all around the place.

"I had bad eyes and kept seeing, target-like circles. After the treatment on my spine and neck, my sight was fine.

"Another time there, I watched them carry a girl in who had slipped on a waxed floor and fell. She couldn't walk in but she did walk out.

"The doctor told me he thought he could have had TB while in Europe." **E. Aro**

"We lived four or five miles beyond the Goat Doctor's. Many times, when walking home from school, people would stop and ask where his place was. I would direct them back to where he was."

E. Personeni

"Carmelita and Frank came over to our house one day in their 1956 International truck. Carmelita was driving. I don't remember ever hearing of or seeing Frank drive. Upon delivering a 25-pound sack of raw sugar he said, *'Train your family to use as little white flour, white sugar and salt as you can, for one of these days, you will see many sicknesses due to these poisonous foods.'*" **E. Kamp**

"A dear, close friend, a motorcycle cop from Palm Springs, could not work or wear the heavy belts with the gun. He came up to the Goat Doctor's and stayed overnight waiting to be treated.

"There would be trailers up and down the road with people staying overnight for help. He had about a twelve-hour wait. After his treatments, he went back to Palm Springs to work and built a large swimming pool!

"My father worked for the fire-fighters in San Bernardino on Interstate 15. He was using a wrench to tighten a bar on the back-up lights on one of the trucks when his back went out. He got treatment from the Goat Doctor and received instant relief."

T. Neeley

"It had taken us hours to get there—we had driven over 90 miles! After waiting our turn, we were asked did we mind if he took this other patient first, because he and his family had been on the road for two days."

D. Brown

"My husband and I lived in Fair Oaks at the time. He was a power lineman for SMUD. Unfortunately, having a history of a bad back, the inevitable day arrived.

"His back went out, to the extent of not being able to stand erectly. He had heard of the Goat Doctor, so we proceeded to go see him.

"When our turn came to the point we could go inside, we sat in a 'waiting room', which was an enclosed unpainted porch. We sat on old chairs and benches. Under those seats were chicken nests from which chickens came and went, as they liked.

"Finally, late in the afternoon, the Doctor came to the door and motioned to my husband to enter. When my husband's treatment was over it was obvious he felt much better, so we left.

"Then he told me that the whole experience was somewhat eerie. When he tried to tell the Goat

278

Doctor his problem, it was evident that he apparently already knew, so his explanations were shrugged off.

"My husband was an extremely muscular man and in the past had suffered through all sorts of rough, ineffective treatment from chiropractors. So he was the most amazed person when he told me about his treatment—soft, gentle manipulation of his arms and legs.

"When the doctor indicated he was through, my husband made the remark that he'd certainly return to him from here on out if he ever had another back problem. The doctor replied, '*I hope to never see you again.*' (This he said countless times—meaning he hoped they stayed well.)

"When my husband asked what he owed, Dr. André replied, 'Whatever you think it was worth!' We didn't have that much money but we were happy to give him more than we had paid chiropractors in the past. Several years later, when my husband did need to see him again, we found he had died."   **L. Oakes**

"A fellow that was working in the Chevrolet garage stepped across the grease pit one day and slipped and fell. He was immobile for three months. The family took him to all different doctors. He was even put in the hospital and put in traction. Nothing and no one seemed to be able to help him.

"Finally, a friend got him into his car, brought him up here to the Goat Doctor's place, and carried him from the car, down the hill, and into the cabin. Frank came out and looked at him and said, 'What seems to be your trouble?'

"The fellow said, 'I can't move my hip.' Frank said, 'I don't think it's your hip.' They got the fellow in the treatment room and laid him on the floor. Frank grabbed one of his legs. He worked it a bit, then he asked the fellow, 'Can you get up and walk?' The fellow did and I watched him walk clear back to the car.

"One time I saw a man all crippled over with what the fellow thought to be arthritis. Frank told him he didn't treat people with diseases, but the best thing he could do for himself would be to get an old tub and fill it with red earth.

"He said, 'Georgetown mud (where the fellow was from) is the best mud in the country and the best thing you can do for your back!' Frank told him to wet it down good, get clear down in, and soak in it. It was best if in the sun."   **M. Pearson**

"Dr. André straightened out my father-in-law's back after he was injured while working on the gold dredge in Natomas. They became good friends.

"Thereafter, my father-in-law would visit him on occasion and take him supplies he needed, usually kerosene.

"One day while working as a lineman for the telephone company, I injured my back. I couldn't walk or stand and had been out of work for an entire month. I'd been to several chiropractors with no improvement. When my father-in-law heard about my situation, he took me to see the Goat Doctor.

"Because Dr. André and my father-in-law were friends, we had gone to the back door of the cabin, knocked, and were let in. Dr. André worked on me in a completely different way from that of the chiropractors I'd been to. He pulled me this way and that, he tugged me that way and this. Then he cranked me every other which way there was left! After that one treatment, I was fine. I've never had another problem with my back."   **W. Langton**

"My dad had a disc that would slip and I used to take him to doctors with one foot dragging, hardly able to walk. One treatment at the Goat Doctor's and he would walk out straight and free from pain.

"I used to pile green lumber in Hazel Valley. Often in the dusk, I would spot the doctor walking to the cemetery or coming back from visiting his mother's gave.

"After the fire happened, Carmelita asked me to come out and search through the rubble for any money. I found a jar full of silver coins, which was all melted together in a glob."   **G. Baraque**

"My mother went there in the 40's and 50's. He told her to put her feet in the mud and to drink carrot juice. She drank so much carrot juice she turned yellow."   **I. Fallon**

"I was 29 years of age when I first went to the goat Doctor. I had a very bad back. I saw him once or twice and he healed me.

"He said he had been in a sanitarium and was given up as a hopeless case and was told he had a short time to live. He told of living with nature, going barefoot, eating the goat meat, and drinking goat milk and was cured by these practices."   **J. Barrett**

"My parents, my brother, and I emigrated from Germany to the United States, in the summer of 1952. About a year after we arrived, my mother experienced very severe back pain that simply would not go away.

"She went to a physician who prescribed some strong pain medication, probably Demerol, but it only treated the symptoms, not the cause. The pain remained, and must have been extreme, because

Mother was not one to complain easily, having had to endure many ailments in her life.

"Neighbors of ours, also German immigrants who had come to America after World War I, saw my mother in pain and inquired about her situation.

"When she explained and said that her treatment by the physician had not brought about any improvement, they told us about the Goat Doctor above Placerville, not far from Roseville, and some of the miraculous stories of his healing successes.

"The stunning thing was the amazing stories we heard from several people about the cures he was able to bring about. People, who had severe illnesses, had lost their speech, were paralyzed for years, and were bedridden or wheelchair-bound, came from far and wide to be treated by him.

"My mother decided to go to him and to let me take her. We had heard about the long lines of people, the fact that many came the night before in order to be at the front of the line, camping out over night and cooking their breakfast over campfires.

"It was a measure of my mother's agonizing pain that she agreed to go at all, since she was really quite nervous about being on the road, much less a treacherous one like this, and with a driver as inexperienced as I was at age 16.

"What we had been told about the Goat Doctor's place and routine turned out to be exactly right. When we arrived before 7:00 a.m., quite a number of people were there ahead of us. Some were cooking breakfast over open fires. We ate some apples and cheese we had brought along and a banana.

"Shortly before 8:00, the Goat Doctor came out of his very modest house, dressed in blue overalls, small bucket in hand, and headed for the wooden shed with the goats.

"Some were bringing loved ones or friends who had been in pain for years in the hope that finally there would be someone who could effect a cure. One family was there from Missouri.

"Around 9 o'clock in the morning, the doctor made his way to his 'office'. The small, simple waiting room was packed, with many more people waiting in the brisk morning air outside. No one pushed. It would have been the wrong thing to do in this peaceful atmosphere of hopeful expectations.

"Dr. André (we didn't know his name then, and everyone simply referred to him as the Goat Doctor) was dressed in clean overalls. He was a man of small stature, perhaps five-foot six inches. He was a quiet person, taciturn, who worked alone, without a receptionist, nurse, or anyone else.

"When it was Mother's turn, she wanted me to go in with her. Mother, not confident yet about her English at the time, thought I could be helpful with translating. That was fine with him.

"We did not know he had been an immigrant from Austria, and thus must have been fluent in German, nor did he mention that or talk German to us, even though my mother and I were conversing in German.

"He asked what the problem was and I explained that she had been having extreme pain in her lower back. He had my mother lie down on his wooden table on her back, fully dressed. It was excruciatingly painful for her to do that.

"He spread a clean, white sheet over her, walked around her, slipped off her shoes, walked back to where her head was, adjusted the shoulders slightly so that she was lying absolutely straight, then walked back to the foot end of the table.

"He pointed out that one of her legs was somewhat shorter than the other and began to manipulate her as a chiropractor would, twisting her this way and that, first pulling one arm while at the same time pushing one leg, then the other leg and arm.

"My mother moaned in pain then let out a little yell. He asked if he was hurting her; she said no, she had just felt a huge pop.

"He said he was finished. My mother got up on her own, still sore, but free of pain. He explained that she had had a flair-up by an old injury and asked her if she had ever had a serious accident long ago. She said that she could not remember. He was sure that the injury had been caused many years ago, judging by the force he had to use in the manipulation.

"Before we left, he asked me if I was having any problems. I said that I was not. He suggested that I lie down on the table anyway. I did.

"He quickly worked on me, and I could hear and feel my bones pop up and down my body, like a zipper. He was done in what seemed to me to be seconds. I can honestly say that I have never physically felt better in my life. I seemed to be sailing through the air rather than walking on the ground.

"We asked what we owed, and he shrugged his shoulders and said we could leave what we liked. I think we left a $20 bill.

"On the way home, we could not talk fast enough about what we had seen, heard, and had experienced ourselves. There was a mystique about the Goat Doctor before we met him, and that had only been reinforced.

"We were eager to tell others about him and to recommend him to people who suffered from painful and paralyzing back and neck problems. His treatment was superb. To my knowledge, my mother's severe back pain never came back, and she lived to be 93.

"I was still puzzled, however, about the 'old injury' the Goat Doctor had diagnosed. My mother said that she could not remember one. When we told my dad about it, he immediately said the injury must have happened 30 years ago when Mother, during their courting days in Germany, had jumped out of a racing horse carriage when Dad had lost control of the galloping horses who had been spooked by a train whistle." **U. H. Hardt, Ph. D.**

"My back and neck were in pain. After hearing my neighbor's stories about him, I decided to see the Goat Doctor. The regular doctors had not helped.

"My Father went into his cabin a cripple and came out walking, carrying his crutches." **J. Hillyard**

"The Goat Doctor had me lay down on his treatment table on my stomach with my left side, arm, leg, and torso on the table and my right side hanging off the table.

"He put his thumb or finger in the nape of my neck somehow, then pulled my right leg that had been hanging up in the air and pushed it hard toward my head. My pain was gone!

"I happened to be there after a treatment when two men came down the hill from the road pushing a woman in a wheelchair. They said the woman, their sister, had been crippled for years. I helped Dr. André and one of the brothers lift the wheelchair patient up the stoop to the house level.

"She was in the treatment room for about 20 minutes when she let out a piercing scream. When her treatment was over, she came out of the room walking. She pushed the wheelchair up the hill to their car. They left as a very happy threesome." **T. Mustra**

"In 1953, I bent over and pinched my sciatic nerve. The pain went down my left leg. I went to a chiropractor, but he was no help. My mother heard of the Goat Doctor from a man who had gone to him and raved to her about him.

"We got there at 8:00 a.m. and were next to the last to be seen at 4:45 p.m. I sat down on a bench in their waiting area, which was an enclosed porch. All of a sudden, a chicken in a box under the bench let out a cackle and laid an egg! It was hysterical!

"There were goatskins all over. It only took 15 to 20 minutes to treat me. I went there three times.

"Frank told me he bought a pair of sandals once a year, he said that was all he needed." **N. Eberhardt**

"I remember Mrs. Andre' predicting the outcome of the war just as it begun." **M. Waggersman**

"I remember seeing Frank, chopping wood in the snow, barefoot. I remember my dad telling me of all the people he saw brought into the cabin in wheelchairs who came out walking." **B. Scott**

"My father had hurt his back at work and continued to have trouble. I was about five years old when my whole family made the trip to see the Goat Doctor. I was intrigued, thinking we were going to see a doctor who was 'half-man, half-goat!'

"I recently asked my father about The Goat Doctor experience and he said the doctor told him he had a slipped pelvic. He said he did a manipulation that was similar to what the chiropractor had done. Father said his treatment didn't make it worse or better.

"He said that his back just gradually seemed to get better by its self, so he didn't really credit the Goat Doctor with the cure.

"Incidentally, I had to stay in the car when my father went in for his treatment, so, I never saw the Goat Doctor during the visit and for years went around imagining him as half-man, half-goat!"

L. Durkee

"I used to have to sit in the car and wait, so I never saw him. I always thought of him as half-man and half-goat."   **G. Schneider**

"We had been in a bad automobile accident. A drunk hit us. The pain was excruciating. I went to several doctors, including two chiropractors and an osteopath. One gave me shots of Novocain in my back. They were of no help so we went to the Goat Doctor.

"It was so strange and there were so many people. There were about 90 goats in the front yard. The goats came first, even if it was your turn.

"He treated me until I was healed. He was an absolute miracle worker and cured me when nothing else worked. My mother went back and told off the two chiropractors.

"I know an awful lot of people from Dobbins, California used to go to him."   **J. Reaves**

"I was a young man of nine when we moved to the Placerville area in 1958. Our property was covered with poison oak. Shortly after our arrival and due to my exploring nature, I came down with a very serious case of the "oozing itch."

"The rash became so serious that I awoke one morning with my PJs stuck to my legs. Out of concern, my mother took me to the local hospital. I was seen by a doctor who soaked the PJs from my legs, then prescribed something to help stop the itching.

"He said that was all he could do and then told my mother to take me to the Goat Doctor and he could help. We did as directed.

"After the Goat Doctor examined me, he told of a way to prevent a reoccurrence of the condition. What he recommended may seem strange, but became a true cure.

"He told us to get an Alpine milk goat and stake it in a poison oak patch so it had to eat the poison oak, and then give me the milk to drink. I was to have no other milk but what came from the goat.

"We had to use soap and warm water to wash the udders of the goat so as not to get a case of poison oak from touching them. From the age of nine until around seventeen, I only drank goat milk.

"I became immune to poison oak and have remained so to the present time. I run a bulldozer and spend a portion of my time clearing property.

"In the course of performing my work, I often run into poison oak. I am so totally immune that on many occasions I have taken the branch of a bush of poison oak and rubbed it on my face and body. Not so much as a bump has resulted.

"On the other hand, my brother, who refused to drink the goat milk due to the so-called taste, continued to be plagued by a severe reaction to poison oak."
R. Stone

"My Aunt and Uncle used to go to the Goat Doctor. She said he always looked at a patient's feet first. Well, my Uncle could be an ornery old codger and didn't like taking his boots off for anyone. But, he would for the Goat Doctor, he thought real highly of him.

"He recommended various teas made from the flowers of the wild daisy, chaparral root, and scotch broom and suggested drinking one quart a day. His skin was as smooth as baby's skin."

"They said he looked like Santa Claus." **E. Smith**

"Just after my third child was born, I suffered from pain in my hip. For seven years, I went to doctors, including a neurologist. I was told I had everything from a pinched nerve to shingles and was treated for each ailment accordingly.

"However, after all the costly and timely treatments, I still had chronic hip pain. One day I was with my parents on a drive, when my father slammed on the brakes to avoid a car that had darted out in front of ours.

"I was tossed off the back seat and somehow dislocated my neck. I was in such pain I couldn't even hold my children. By now, I had heard of the miraculous Goat Doctor. I had been so discouraged with the doctors I had been to, so I decided to go to him instead.

"While standing behind me, he used his knee as well as his hands. He did an adjustment that didn't hurt at all. Within 15 seconds, my neck injury was corrected. Then he had me lay on his treatment table. He proceeded to check the rest of my body from head to toe. I had not mentioned my bad hip. It had been something I had lived with for so long. He suddenly took the leg on my bad hip side and started to rotate my leg off that side of the table.

"I barely got the words out of my mouth, 'Oh please don't ----.' I was trying to tell him I was so afraid anything could make it worse.

"Before I could finish, he had completed what he had set out to do. He fixed my hip that quick! He then had me stand up and walk.

"I was absolutely amazed. My neck and hip pain were totally gone. Don't ask me how! His hands were so soft and yet very strong. From that day to this, I've never had a neck or hip pain. I continued seeing Dr. André through the years. He told me he was not a spiritual healer. He knew the anatomy of the body.

"In visiting Dr. André, I particularly remember a young girl whom I had seen there before. Each time she would hobble down from the road to the cabin with crutches.

"After her visit with Dr. André, she came out walking on her own, with someone else carrying the crutches. I asked Dr. André about her.

"He explained to me that the girl had polio. He said she came regularly, once a month. He would give her a treatment in which he stretched her muscles. She would get relief for several days.

"After that, she regressed as the muscles tightened up again. He said that as long as she had such a treatment, until she matured into adulthood when her bones stopped growing, she would then be fine.

"She had been given no hope by her prior doctors and was even told she would have no children. She did heal completely and has a lovely family.

"In describing Dr. André's looks now, I think he looked like a miniature Kenny Rogers and he was always spotless."   **J. Hutchins**

"A friend of mine had a baby girl through a difficult birth. The baby cried a lot and kept the parents awake all night, every night. She just would not sleep. Their doctor just said, 'a lot of babies cry a lot'. He gave them a prescription for some kind of medicine that made her act sluggish.

"Someone told them about the goat doctor being a miracle worker who could cure just about anything. They went to him. They entered the treatment room intending to explain their problem, but as soon as they walked in, the Goat Doctor put his arms out and said, 'Give me that baby'.

"For about a half an hour, he gently massaged her little body, turning her over, and back, several times. That was all he appeared to do. When he was through, he told them, 'Don't ever give her drugs again!'

"My friend told me their little girl slept all the way home and has never had any problems sleeping from that day on."   **E. Clark**

"I knew Frank in the 1950's for approximately six years. We had a nice chat the last time I saw him. I was delivering a pickup load of goats to him. He was low on his, as he had sold off quite a bit of goat meat. He only had twenty-five to thirty goats left so he was real happy to get them.

"He would fix my back whenever I had it go out on me. One visit always took care of it. I'd go for sometime and then do something to put it out, but it stayed good for months at a time.

"My Uncle had been injured in the San Francisco quake. He went to Doc André but Frank told him he could not help him. His injuries were permanent. He said it would be better to leave it alone or it could be damaged further."   **G. Dean**

"We'd take a picnic and make a day of it. When he treated me, it felt like he had no bones in his hands—they were so soft."   **M. Crozer**

"In 1955, I went to him for treatment for my bad back. It was of no help. While I was there, I gave one of his patients an IV of Demerol prior-to manipulation.

"He was sort of on the mystic side. He was honest and if he couldn't help you, he said to see an M. D."

Dr. L.E. Shortes

"When Frank got so overly busy and it was such a long trip to his place, Frank showed me an adjustment to do on our friend Bill. He even drew up plans for me to make an exact replica of his treatment table which I still have." **W. Durfey**

"As neighbors, I saw him often. I used to meet him now and again while walking along the road.

"One day when I was a freshman, I was wearing a beautiful straw hat, André told me to push my hat back off my head. He told me I would do well in whatever I wanted to do.

"André told me he didn't believe in shots, it was just putting poison in your system. It was his mother who took care of the finances." **L. Croft**

"I used to take my wife out there for treatment and the Goat Doctor used to get after me about my smoking." **G. Wigglesworth**

"The Goat Doctor had been pointed out to me in a grocery store, and of course, I was curious about him, from all the weird things I had heard.

"A friend of mine hurt his back and couldn't work. The family was in dire straits. They were desperate. He asked me if I could take him to see the Goat Doctor.

"My friend came out standing straight and tall. He was convinced that the Goat Doctor was the best and went back many times after that for help with ulcers, bad back, and whatever else ailed him. That was quite an experience." **A. Williams**

"I worked for Placerville Lumber Company. When the men would get their backs out of shape, and those who went for conventional methods of treatment paid by their insurance, were off work for many weeks in traction with a great deal of pain and expense.

"Those who went to Dr. André and paid their three dollars were usually back to work the next day minus pain and no expense to the insurance company.

"Finally, the insurance company got smart and said they would cover Dr. André. Boy did they save money! Placerville Lumber Company saved too, because the men got right back to the job." **L. Phipps**

"I stooped over to pick up a bucket and my back went out in the upper area. My back and shoulders were in pain. The doctor had me sit on a short stool. He put his knee to my back and had me swing my arms slowly back and forth.

"All of a sudden, I felt a feeling of easement and comfort. My husband went to him after that. He asked when he should come back and the doctor said, 'only return if you need me'. He really helped him.

"One day Dr. André said, 'There will come a time, I won't be here for you.' He died shortly after. I think he knew his time was up." **B. Rommel**

"When I was 28 years of age, my horse fell and rolled over on me. I went only once to the Goat Doctor and was told that he didn't think he could help me because of the condition of my body. He also told me about the poisons of smoking.

"Then he took me in to see his mother who told me a lot of things about myself that no one else knew.

"There are still some of the goats from his herd, that have become wild, in the area."   **T. Sigwart**

"After my uncle, Lewis Dick, died, I inherited his property. There was a shed on his land. When I opened the door, I was surprised to see boxes of Zane Grey novels.

"The first time I went there I was surprised to see white peacocks! There were regular ones too; I'd say half a dozen."   **M. Badeker**

"One day my brother and I were playing cowboys. I was on his hands and knees playing "horse" to my brother's "cowboy." My brother accidentally hurt me when he jumped up and down on my back, kicked me in the ribs and yelled "Giddiup!'

"I was seven years old and partially crippled when my mother took me to a chiropractor who lived next door to us in Nevada City. Several visits did not help.

"Then she took me to another chiropractor, who worked in Grass Valley five miles away.

"Then she took me to see an orthopedist. That doctor told her one of my ankles was lower than the other one and the heel of one shoe would have to be raised and the inside of both shoes would have to be built up to accommodate where my feet turned in.

"He told her I would need special shoes and braces to get by and would be partially crippled for the rest of his life.

"He fitted me for braces and shoes. They looked very much like the shoes and braces worn in the movie Forest Gump. They were expensive and much more than my mother could afford. So she told him she would have to wait a while and think about it.

"A short time later a friend happened to mention to my Mother something about a "Miracle Worker" over by Placerville, called the "Goat Doctor." I consider it lucky that she didn't have the money or she would have bought the stuff and we wouldn't have gone to Mosquito.

"I remember wondering, 'Why are we going to a goat doctor and not a human doctor?'

"After waiting our turn, we entered the treatment room and were introduced to Dr. André by a female assistant. While helping me onto the treatment table, the doctor greeted us by saying, 'What do we have here?'

"My mother told how I had come running to her crying after accidentally getting hurt while playing with my brother. The doctor checked the length of each of my legs, then barely touched my back before saying, 'It may well be that it hurt when his brother bumped him, but his original injury occurred when he fell off the roof of a garage'.

"The things he did seemed not so different from what the other chiropractors did, but he didn't scare me and it didn't hurt. It was a one-shot cure that he did almost as fast as the snap of the fingers.

"As he helped me off his table, Dr. André said to my mother and grandmother, 'I think he'll be just fine now,' in a reassuring and very confident voice.

"After caring for me, the doctor looked at my Mother and said, 'Would you like to have a treatment?" She said, 'Oh, no, I just brought Gordy for you to take care of.

"He looked at her somewhat sternly and said, ' I think you should have a treatment'. As soon as he touched her when laying her down on his table, he said, 'You have an old problem, in your neck, from an accident you were in. It has been that way so long I can't make it right, but I can make it better.'

"'You may have forgotten this because it happened 11 years ago, but it's still causing you problems.' Mother thought back for a moment and then said, 'You know, you're right. About 11 years ago I was in nurse's training. I was riding in a Greyhound bus that was rear-ended by a diesel truck and my neck hurt for three weeks.'

"My grandmother, a religious scholar who was always looking for any sign of the devil anywhere, asked, 'How do you know that?'

"Dr. André didn't realize what she was up to and said offhandedly, 'When I touch someone I know what's wrong with them.' Then my grandmother, her voice fairly dripping with suspicion and accusation said, 'How do you do that?'

"The Goat Doctor by now had figured out where she was coming from. He turned toward her with a face that became luminous and seemed to glow with righteousness and said, 'It's a gift from God.'

"My grandmother just stopped still and didn't move or say anything, like she was petrified by the experience of seeing him that way. She never even hinted anything but good about the Goat Doctor from then on.

"I immediately went back to being the impetuously wild active child I had been before. Although, I did have to go back once or twice a year when I did something that put it out again.

"Eventually, I wrestled on the school teams at Colfax High School, Sierra College and the University of California at Santa Barbara. While running track at Colfax, I held the school record in the two-mile run for a few years and ran cross-country at Sierra.

"In 1971 and '72, I rode in the Western States Trail Ride on a mongrel horse, changing to a purebred horse in 1973 thinking it would be faster, but the horse went lame.

"By that time, I was doing marathon running and had the fastest time ever run by someone who weighed over 200 pounds. So I left the horse at home

Gordon Ainsleigh, D. C. (courtesy of C. Barieau)

in 1974 and ran the whole race on foot in 23 hours and 47 minutes, thus starting the 50 and 100-mile ultra-marathon trail running events.

"I was the first person in modern history to run 100 miles in 24 hours over trails through mountains and canyons. I have run nineteen 100-mile runs in California, Utah, Colorado, and Vermont as of 1999. I am, also, an accomplished rock climber.

"I owe my success to Dr. André. He took my life and turned it around. I was destined to be deformed and with braces like a real life Forrest Gump. He did an awful lot of good for an awful lot of people. He is still my guiding light."   **G. Ainsleigh, D.C.**

"One day, not long after starting my practice in Placerville, a little old man came into the office all bent-over in pain. He became real feisty when I told him I felt he should be x-rayed.

"He said, 'Look, I don't need no x-rays, I just want an adjustment like ole Doc André gave me that's all.' He continued running off at the mouth about this so-called miracle man, alternating between calling him 'ole Doc André' or the Goat Doctor" and how he fixed him up just fine with one treatment that lasted him 25 years.

"With patients in the waiting room listening to all this, I became upset with him and for a minute-or-two felt like grabbing him by the scruff of the neck and tossing him out the door.

"He continued harping on about this "Miracle Man" as I went about giving him a treatment, until, I'm not quite sure when it was, he grasped my attention.

"I just know that by the time we were through, I had told the party who brought him to me, that they could leave and I would drive him home.

"This was because he lived near the Goat Doctor's old property and I was now so interested in all he told me about the man, not only did I want to hear more about him, I wanted very much to see the place where his miraculous work took place.

"From there, my patient had me drive over to the Goat Doctor's good friend, Lois Pearson, so she could tell me more about him. I have continued from that day to this to be interested in hearing more about the man."   **M. Yablonovsky, D.C.**

In Memory of Frank Andre:

"When Dr. André was a young man, he contracted tuberculosis and was given two months to live. This was told to me by my husband, and later, by Dr. André.

"Dr. André felt that God and Jesus had given him his healing powers. I believe this was true. He lived by Christ's teaching, devoting his life to people. He tried so hard to cure and heal every soul that came to him. He helped thousands of people. I remember him as being the kindest man I have ever known. May God bless his gentle soul."   **D. Randon**

"Not a month goes by that I don't think of him. I feel Frank André inspired me to live my life as a kinder and more caring individual."   **J. Roberts**

"No one could ever forget Frank. He was someone special and apart—he was beautiful inside and out. He always said his healing was a gift of God, a power over and above his. Well, he was a gift from God and every one who knew him, loved him."   **V. Alexander**

"I could go on for hours about him. I knew him intimately for five years. His hands were his heart and soul."   **A. Boeding**

"One thing that stands out in my memories of the Goat Doctor is the way his skin appeared—so thin and taut on the bones of his fingers that they could come right through the skin at any time. It looked like if you were to try to push a stick through a sponge that was all worn out, there was no flesh; it was as though he had worked away all the meat on

---

his fingers after so many years of massaging so many people." **C. Gemmet**

"I always thought the most of him. He was a very gifted person and the finest man I ever knew. He was a Christ like figure—a giving person to be on this planet to help people. He had to-have-been-touched by God in some manner for all he did to have worked out so well. I consider myself very fortunate that he was part of my life." **O. Beckett**

"He was a gentle, honest, and humble individual. He seemed to have an inner strength." **G. McKee**

"He lived by Christ's teachings, devoting his life to people. I do so hope the Lord will remember those two good people (Frank and Anna) when he goes over the list of those sacred." **E. M. Bliss**

"Dear Dr. André inspired me in my living habits. He dedicated his life to compassionate service and deep charity to all people, I thought so highly of him." **E. Kamp**

"He may not have had a formal education to have earned a certificate that denoted his having been approved by the State Medical Board, but except for a few good friends who called him Frank, he was and still is called Dr. André. The respect and reverence that comes from those who knew him, is as strong as ever. He touched a lot of lives." **C. Neilsen**